Half the House

Half the House

20th Anniversary Edition

a memoir

Richard Hoffman

With a new introduction by Louise DeSalvo

Many Americas
Rediscovery Series

New Rivers Press
c/o MSUM
1104 7th Avenue South
Moorhead, MN 56563
www.newriverspress.com

Copyright © 2015 by Richard Hoffman
Copyright © 2005 by Richard Hoffman
Postscript © 2005 by Richard Hoffman

Originally published by Harcourt Brace & Company, 1995

Epigraph from Savidis, George, ed. C.P. Cavafy: Collected Poems, rev. ed. © 1975, 1992 by Edmund Keeley and Philip Sherrard, transl. Reprinted by permission of Princeton University Press.

Library of Congress Control Number: 2014958825
ISBN: 978-0-89823-339-1

Cover design: Amanda Ketterling
Author photograph: Thom Harrigan
Introduction design: Daniel Arthur Shudlick

The publication of *Half the House, 20th Anniversary Edition* is made possible by the generous support of Minnesota State University Moorhead, The McKnight Foundation, the Dawson Family Endowment, and other contributors to New Rivers Press.

For academic permission please contact Frederick T. Courtright at 570-839-7477 or permdude@eclipse.net.

New Rivers Press is a nonprofit literary press associated with Minnesota State University Moorhead.

Alan Davis, Co-Director and Senior Editor
Suzzanne Kelley, Co-Director and Managing Editor
Wayne Gudmundson, Consultant
Thom Tammaro, Poetry Editor
Kevin Carollo, MVP Poetry Coordinator
Vincent Reusch, MVP Prose Coordinator
Nayt Rundquist, Assistant Production Editor

Printed in the United States of America

Many Americas Rediscovery Series

New Rivers Press
c/o MSUM
1104 7th Avenue South
Moorhead, MN 56563
www.newriverspress.com

*For my family, living and dead,
but especially for my father*

The author wishes to thank Tom D'Evelyn, Linda McCarriston, and Martha Ramsey for their help. A special thanks is due to Dick Lourie for his sound editorial advice.

My deepest gratitude is reserved for my dearest friend, Kathleen Aguero, my wife, my colleague, my love, who brought her powerful insight, empathy, and wisdom to bear on every word in this book. In every way imaginable she is a blessing upon my life.

This is not a work of fiction.
It contains no composite characters,
no invented scenes. I have, in most instances,
altered the names of persons outside my family.
In one instance, on principle, I have not.

GROWING IN SPIRIT

He who hopes to grow in spirit
will have to transcend obedience and respect.
He will hold to some laws
but he will mostly violate
both law and custom, and go beyond
the established, inadequate norm.
Sensual pleasures will have much to teach him.
He will not be afraid of the destructive act:
half the house will have to come down.
This way he will grow virtuously into wisdom.

C.P. Cavafy

INTRODUCTION

"Our Life"
On the Twentieth Anniversary Edition of Richard Hoffman's
Half the House

I.

All the writers I know hope their work will make a difference in their readers' lives. But the book in your hands—the twentieth anniversary edition of Richard Hoffman's *Half the House*—has had an enormous impact on many people's lives, especially many young boys' lives. Ironically, we and these young boys will never know who they are, because Hoffman wrote—in graphic detail—how he was raped by Tom Feifel, a football and baseball coach in Allentown, Pennsylvania, Hoffman's home town; and because Hoffman's father put his son's published memoir into the hands of a friend who gave it to the mothers of boys Feifel was currently coaching; and because, as a result, it was learned that Feifel was *still* molesting boys all these years after he'd assaulted Hoffman and had been continuing to do so during his forty-year career as a coach. Only then was Feifel arrested, charged, convicted, and incarcerated. And so, Feifel was prevented from continuing his premeditated, systematic program of finding victims and raping them.

As significant as Feifel's punishment may be—and it certainly is, for justice's sake—even more important is the fact that Feifel's incarceration stopped him from adding even one more boy to the more than four hundred boys he'd already victimized.

Yes, more than four hundred boys.

Hoffman's forthrightness in telling his story—which was not his story alone, but that of all those other boys, too, although he didn't know about them when he was writing and could never have imagined the number of boys Feifel had abused—prevented many children whom Feifel had likely already singled out, from being raped. (Hoffman has in his possession a chilling photograph Feifel took of him and other members of the baseball team he coached. Penned on the photo is a very large arrow pointing directly to Hoffman. "This is the one," the handwriting says.) *Half the House* has permitted an untold number of boys to live a child's life untrammeled by the consequences of sexual abuse that Hoffman relates in his narrative. Or so we hope.

Not that this achievement diminishes Hoffman's pain, described with enormous empathy for his younger and present self in these pages, nor the pain of those more than four hundred children. The aftereffects of such trauma are enormous, are consequential, and live on. Still, through the act of bearing witness to what happened to him as a boy, Hoffman has engaged in that most ethical of human acts: the act of bearing witness to the suffering self. And our reading Hoffman's *Half the House* demands of us an equally essential ethical act: that of bearing witness to the suffering of another; that of allowing that witness to show us what he believes is the largest possible meaning of what happened to him in the context of his personal and his nation's history: what can become of boys in a culture like our own.

II.

Half the House isn't only a memoir about one sex offender, one boy, or even the more than four hundred boys who were Feifel's victims, although if it were only that, it would be more than enough. *Half the House* is not only that "sex abuse memoir," as newspapers sometimes labeled it after its initial publication. And it's not just about Hoffman's family, although the memoir tells us so very much about his family's life in a working class blue collar Catholic household (and working class life in the United States); his childhood before Feifel singled him out and began raping him; the hard manual labor of Hoffman's father to support his family; the thwarted dreams of working class people whose labor is not respected for what it is—the necessary adhesive that holds the fabric of our lives together; the lives of his brothers, two of whom died young from muscular dystrophy, and what it takes for a poor family to care for their children without the help that only far more money than what they have can buy; the life of his mother—her endurance in the face of enormous difficulty, and its cost to her. And how the family carries on. And how it carries on.

III.

When a radio interviewer tried to diminish the significance of *Half the House* by trying to cast it as Hoffman's idiosyncratic story, and when she had the temerity to suggest that writing the book had made everything better for Hoffman, had been an act of "catharsis" for him, the meaning of which she grossly misunderstood, Hoffman rebutted, "My book is not about my life . . . My book is about *our* life." For *Half the House* reframes boyhood in the United States as a period during which boys are systematically taught to become violent, or to become victims of violence, or both. A period during which they are routinely abased and abused, often through organized sports, often under the guise of toughening them up for their own good.

Feifel demanded that his charges drive out their empathy. He taught them to distrust one another; to compete with one another; to turn on each other; to beat each other; to—literally—piss on the weakest amongst them; to send those who could not withstand and tolerate all this violence flailing towards self-blame, self-abuse, and self-destruction.

Again, this is not Hoffman's life. It is our life. It is what we allow. It is what we witness, what we all too often do so very little to stop. Absent the sexual violence, how Feifel treated the boys in his charge is how our culture treats so many of its boys, so many of its children, so that Feifel's sexual victimization of the more than four hundred children enacts in its most horrifying form the ritual of dominance and submission in our culture. It is our life.

IV.

"Hit him again. Hit him again. Harder. Harder."

This call to violence was shouted by cheerleaders standing along the sidelines of a football field in 1959 in Ridgefield, New Jersey, the town where I grew into adolescence.

"Hit him again. Hit him again. Harder. Harder."

V.

Any time I teach memoir writing, any time I read a memoir, I must remember that these writers aren't just sharing their stories with me and with others; they are sharing what *happened* to them, what *really happened* to them. They share what they are making of the meaning of their lives. In the literary memoir, when the writer speaks of rape, or violence, or torture, it is not just a narrative, not just a story. It is a retelling of the writer's life shaped and formed into a work of art so that the reader can witness what has transpired and we can begin to understand (though never fully) what has happened to the writer, and the meaning the writer has made of it.

And so it becomes our story, too. We can understand what happened to us because the writer—as Hoffman does in these pages—has so eloquently described what happened to him.

Hence, the attack on memoir. The regarding of it as a second-class genre.

Memoir is dangerous. Memoir so often dares to tell what people would prefer not to know.

VI.

Fourteen years. This is the number of years it took Richard Hoffman to write *Half the House*. He has spoken to me of how he began the work to try to come to terms with what happened to him. The work began as a novel, even as a revenge fantasy against Feifel. But he was also beginning to write a memoir—a narrative of his family's life. He believed, initially, that these were two stories, two books. But a friend told him they were the same story—the thread of understanding the nature of oppression, among other themes, unites them—and that he would have to find a way to integrate them. Each, alone, was not the whole story. The narratives, interleaved, would become that story that would be *our* story.

Hoffman knew he had to work slowly. He would write. And then walk away from the writing. He would write. And then stop writing.

He had, he said, spent years hiding things in cupboards in his psyche. As an image emerged, he would follow it where it took him. But it might be a year before he could access something else. So that by writing about a snippet of memory, Hoffman unlocked his past piece by piece, bit by bit. Ultimately, the process of completing the work became a huge job of assembling the fragments. Hoffman took the pieces, affixed them to the walls of his workroom, and assembled and reassembled them, finding the links in the narrative as he ordered and organized.

Although Hoffman said he wasn't sure whether the work would save him or kill him, he discovered, in time, that in the process of making *Half the House*, he was fighting for a sense of wholeness that "only that process could give me."

VII.

In 1880 or thereabouts, Roger Fry, then still a boy, who, in his adulthood was a member of the Bloomsbury group and a prominent artist and art critic, wrote a series of letters home to his mother, Lady Fry, from Sunninghill House, the school he was currently attending. Fry had been sent there specifically because its head, a Mr. Sneyd-Kynnersley, avowed that at this school there would be no punishments.

In one letter, Fry recounts that two boys are bullying him "as much as they can, sometimes by teasing, and sometimes by hitting me about." But their favorite form of torture, he relates, was holding him under water (a childhood version of waterboarding). And their favorite form of abuse was "upset[ting]" Fry when he bathed.

Fry described the numerous floggings he witnessed. As a head boy, he was required to hold the victim down while Sneyd-Kynnersley (he who professed there would be no beatings) whipped them. Although Fry told his mother how he was bullied and how severe the beatings were, Fry's parents did not interfere. They did not put a stop to what Fry aptly refers to as Sneyd-Kynnersley's "executions."

Years later, Fry wrote an unexpurgated version of his life at Sunninghill that Virginia Woolf quotes in her biography of him. Woolf wanted to expose the violence against boys that she believed was at the heart of British culture. What better way than to use his own words? In *Three Guineas*, which she'd published a few years before, she connected this violence against boys to violence against women, to war, to colonialism, just as Hoffman connects violence against boys to so many patterns of oppression in our own culture. And Woolf maintained that it was useless to fight dictators and their abuses abroad unless we are willing to "crush him in our own country." Unless this happened, she believed that the abuses of the powerful against the weak would continue to govern and contaminate the lives of women, children, and the powerless.

VIII.

Twenty years after the initial publication of *Half the House*, Richard Hoffman still gets letters and e-mails from people all over the world. They thank him for his book. They tell him that his work has helped them unlock the secrets of their own past, and that through reading about his life, they have learned much about their own. And this new edition will bring scores more readers to this essential work, will help these readers understand their own lives, will inspire several to write their own empathic accounts of self-witness. For *Half the House* is, as Richard Hoffman has said, not only his life, but our life, too.

Louise DeSalvo

—author of *Writing as a Way of Healing*
and *The Art of Slow Writing*

chapter one
1984

"IT ALL DEPENDS how deep your brothers are buried," my father said. We were sitting at the kitchen table and he was taking papers from a gray steel box, removing fat red rubber bands, sorting things into piles. "Somewhere I have a deed. The Sacred Heart allows double burial, at least that's what old Mary Becker told me years ago. But you have to go down seven feet with the first one. Where's my glasses? Here. No, that's not it. We'll have to see how deep your brothers Mike and Bob are buried."

Aunt Kitty, my father's sister, came into the kitchen and went to the windowsill over the sink where we kept my mother's medications. "You two ought to get some rest. I'm all right with her for now." She was holding the vial of pills in one hand and adjusting her glasses with the other, peering at the label. "Dare she have another one of these so soon I wonder."

"Give it to her if she wants one," my father said. "It don't make no difference now. Here," he said to me, sliding the metal box across the table, "see if you can find anything from the Becker Funeral Home or the Sacred Heart Cemetery."

"Wait," I said to my aunt; she was filling a glass with water at the sink. "She can't take them like that. You have to crush them in sherbet."

"Shit!" My father reached for his wallet. "Quick!" he said, handing me a wad of bills. "Run up to the corner and get some more sherbet." I took the money from him, saw it was about thirty dollars, and peeled off three singles. "This is enough," I said. He was already walking away; he waved his hand. "Who gives a shit. Buy ten. Buy twenty. It'll just go to the fuckin' doctors anyway."

Aunt Kitty touched me on the back of the neck so I would know to say nothing. Dad went into the living room, where he'd built a smaller room in the front by the window for my mother; like the one we'd built years earlier for my brothers, it was made of two-by-fours and cheap panelling. There was a shower curtain over the narrow doorway. I saw him go in. I heard him say, quietly, "How're you feeling, sweetheart?"

That small room where my mother died is gone now. The rented hospital bed faced the large front window; hanging plants obstructed the view of the street. The top of the window is leaded and stained glass, deep purples alternating with tulips of opaque swirled cream and frosted panels. Heavy drapes, closed at sunset, were opened each morning at the first rumor of dawn. Generally, during her last weeks, my mother slept little, and then only in the morning when she saw the window brighten again. Her bed was placed along one of the makeshift walls so that one of the two-by-fours served as a narrow shelf beside her for a box of tissues, her inhaler, a jar of Vaseline. Next to the gurgling oxygen compressor, her night table held her alarm clock and two pictures of her infant grandson, Robert, my son.

It is a mere accident of time that my mother began to die so soon after her first grandchild was born, but the irony of it produced such pain that it sometimes seemed to me that all of nature had conspired to torture us. During her last days, among the things my mother whispered to no one in particular was, "Not now. Oh, please, not now."

I left to buy the sherbet, using the back door so I wouldn't disturb my parents. I could hear my mother crying, my father soothing her, my mother saying something in a hoarse whisper. By then I had learned not to intrude.

THE CHRISTMAS BEFORE, my wife and I came across something in a card shop called "Grandma's Book." The pages, illustrated like a children's book, were headed with questions. "What was your favorite subject in school? Where did you live when you were growing up? How did you meet my grandpa?" Kathi made it easier for me by buying one for her mother too. The store had no "Grandpa's Book," so I bought two notebooks into which I copied all the questions, in different colored inks, and pasted in humorous pictures from magazines, an alligator next to "Did you have any pets when you were a boy?," a log cabin next to "What kind of house did you grow up in?" All this effort was of course to keep from singling out my mother. All to keep her from thinking we'd given up hope. We had. And she was never fooled. The book is blank.

A T THE FUNERAL parlor, Dad was dissatisfied. "She never stuck out her jaw like that. That's not right." He wanted me to share again in his outrage.

"It doesn't matter, Dad. This isn't Mom. Mom's gone."

He sighed through his nose and gave me a look both disappointed and angry.

I was wrong.

I went forth from my mother's body and, the eldest son, I had traveled far from her. My father disciplined himself, as husband and father, lover, to come back to her body, always, back to the body of his love. His grimace was a measure of the gulf between us.

"Dolly," he said, touching her hands. He shook his head and wept.

And I understood my mother's death was not our common loss.

chapter two

1984

FOR MANY YEARS my mother's hair was lacquered blacker than it was when she was young. Once she was embarrassed when I came home from college a couple of days early and she hadn't gotten to the salon and her roots were showing. Shame, that goes to the roots: my mother bore two congenitally ill, doomed sons. For her, muscular dystrophy was a mythic curse: only males are afflicted by it, and only females carry it. A genetic defect. I can imagine my mother washing her face in the morning, looking at herself in the mirror, protecting herself, vigilant against the gray or silk-white roots that prove the past, that say that time is once, once, once. For so many years she knew her sons would die before her that she had to deny time every day to be there for them, to feed them, wash them, bring them books, papers and pencils, change the channel, bring the pisspot. Michael screamed in the night most every night for five or six years, waking everyone. She slept in a chair downstairs so she could wake him faster from his nightmares. How could she possibly believe one lifetime is all there is? She went to the cemetery, often. She had kept them alive inside her once before. "We'll be together again someday," she would insist, holding up her index finger. "Nobody can say it's not true."

MY MOTHER ALWAYS corrected people who thought that Dolly was short for Dolores; then she'd tell a story. "When the nurse handed me to my mother, all wrapped up in a blanket, my mother bent over me and said, 'Oh, you little doll . . . eeeee!'" She cried out in mock horror as if the little "doll" were so ugly as to produce the shrieked second syllable of her name.

My brother Joe took a Polaroid family picture the Christmas before my mother's death. We passed it around and as we emerged, as if from a mist, my mother placed her thumb over her face and said, "Nice picture."

When she was younger, my mother's discomfort with herself might have been mistaken for vanity. I remember her sitting at the kitchen table in a white satin robe and slippers, smoking, rolling her hair into flat curls she fastened with bobby pins. The robe had an iridescent pattern that made me think it was made of very thinly sliced wood. I'd seen that same kind of pattern on the shiny chasuble our pastor, Father Walters, wore at Mass. I must have been about four years old. I was interested in people's clothing. I thought people chose to do the things they did so they could wear the costume they wanted to wear. Firemen agreed to fight fires so they could wear firemen's hats and boots. If you were happiest in a gray denim cap and red neckerchief, the thing to do was learn to drive a train.

I remember playing on the light-green linoleum of the kitchen floor, coloring and talking to my mother and sometimes to myself. She sat sideways at the table, leaning forward to pluck her eyebrows with tweezers, peering into a round mirror she held in her other hand. Sometimes her concentration was so fierce it was hard for me to penetrate her solitude. The mirror made things look bigger. The other end of the tweezers had a hole in it which she pressed against her forehead, her cheeks, her chin. It left red circles all over her face. She kept wiping the end of the tweezers on a tissue she held in her hand along with the mirror. It looked like she was hurting herself. A lipstick-tipped Chesterfield burned in a heavy glass ashtray.

"But what *are* blackheads?" I asked.

"They're ugly, that's what they are." A drag on the Chesterfield. Squinting through smoke. Exasperation at the curl that had unwound from its bobby pin. "Leave me alone now. Draw me a nice picture or something."

My memories of these kitchen evenings are vivid, and I suspect that there was a particular night of the week when my father took my brother Bob with him and left me with my mother and her magnifying mirror. Probably those times I spent alone with my father—walking uptown to look in the store windows, or walking through the cemetery with its urns and angels, squirrels and muzzled cannons—were nights when Bob stayed home and maybe wondered at my mother's fierce impatience with herself. I don't know.

I remember an earthquake no one else recalls. It was a summer night, moths bumping against the screen door, lightning bugs blinking in the yard. I was lying on the cool linoleum floor. I have a vague memory of having done something wrong. I had been crying, probably throwing a tantrum on the floor, when I felt the house begin to shake. The screen door opened and closed and a moth flew in, in just that space of time. There was a low rumbling and trembling. My father said something about an earthquake and went to call the Pennsylvania Power & Light Co. My mother, in her satin robe, held me on her slippery lap. Bob may have been there too. I don't remember. No one else remembers any of this. Over the years, whenever I'd bring it up, my mother always said, "Get the hell out. An earthquake? You're dreaming."

MY MOTHER'S VOICE—her "Dutch" accent, is hard to render on the page. The pitch and lilt of the Pennsylvania Dutch accent is, I think now, beautiful for its tone of innocent questioning, the voice generally swelling once about mid-sentence before concluding like a question even when it isn't. And for the integrity of its stubbornly German syntax. I didn't always think so, however, and remembering the years I spent as a young man trying to shed that inflected speech, I am struck by how pervasive was my mother's influence on me, not to mention the persistence of her shame. She was stuck between not wanting to talk "Dutchified" and not wanting to sound "citified," which she was afraid would be construed as putting on airs.

My mother taught me to devalue her. Even that sentence —let it stand—blames her for everything, including the shame I feel for having been ashamed of her. I grew up watching which fork others were using, what they were wearing, what they were talking about, what they seemed to be thinking. They, whoever they happened to be, had the power to find us wanting. "I'm not going to take you anywhere anymore unless you learn how to behave."

The only picture I have of my mother as a child has

been literally defaced: she scratched out her face with something sharp and scribbled over it with a red crayon. I asked her about it once. She avoided telling me why she did it. "Boy, did I get a lickin' for that," was all she said.

Between 1970 and 1972, my mother lost her mother and two of her sons: first Mike, then Mammy Etta, then Bob. Careful to hide her bitterness, she went deep inside herself and stayed there, at the same time constructing some other person to present to us, someone who was cheerfully busy, brimming with jokes, gossip, idle chatter. It was as if she herself were absent, but had created some rough replica through which she attempted to go on with her life. I pretended not to see this, played along with it; I believe we all did. She'd tell the same jokes over and over, sometimes within the same conversation. She'd talk about the rising price of peas or lettuce, and if the conversation lagged, she'd repeat herself, sometimes in exactly the same words.

"I'd planned on making pork chops, but they were awfully high—last week they were two eighty-nine and now they're up to three forty-nine. It's just ridiculous. . . . Oh, Marietta told me a good one last week: this guy goes into a bar and . . . I'm going to put some onions in with the roast; you always liked that. . . . I can't believe it, what they're getting for pork chops. . . ."

Occasionally, however, she would hint at what was really going on inside her, but in a way that discouraged further conversation. Sometimes she talked about Henry, the grocer in our old neighborhood who'd committed suicide. She mentioned him many times and always asked if I remembered. Of course. He and my mother had a secret that intrigued and mystified me when I was a kid. I often went to the store for my mother after school, before I was allowed to play. Sometimes my mother instructed me to see Henry, no one else; I was to ask for "a box of jiggers." There was something mysterious, perhaps forbidden, going on. When I asked Henry about it, he said, "Never you mind," in a way that made my imagination flare and strain to think what they could be. He had to get them down from the highest shelf with a caliper on a long stick; it was a light blue box with a pink rose on it. By the second grade I could read enough to sound out the words and sometimes guess at the meanings. I knew what a napkin was, and sanitary meant something about dirt or toilets, I wasn't sure. I had to know.

I got my candy money by collecting empty bottles around the neighborhood, two cents for the small ones and five cents for the big ones, and when I had enough I went to see Henry. I ran two blocks to a lot behind the Presbyterian church and tore open the box. They were white, with cotton squares like the bottom of jewelry boxes, sealed with a tissue like Kleenex, and with a little blue stripe down the middle. I thought they must be bandages. Not long after that, I found one in the garbage can, bloody, covered with flies. They *were* bandages. I had figured out the secret: *My mother was hurt, wounded, but she was too brave to tell us.*

chapter three

1956

IN THE MORNING, Bob and I would wake in our bed and laugh and fight. If he woke before me, he would nudge me, poke me, kick me, and if all else failed, open my eyelids with his fingers, asking, "Dick, are you awake yet?"

I remember hanging my foot out from the covers on a morning when I could see my breath, pinching my nose shut to keep from laughing, seeing how long I could stand it, letting my foot get colder and colder, intent on how he would shriek when I placed it on his sleeping back, anticipating his counterattack and readying my pillow for a shield. Mom would be in to wake us any minute, and when I heard her on the stairs I did it, right up under the back of his pajama top.

"Hey! Quit it! Quit it! Mom!"

"Let's go, you two monkeys. Time to get up!"

Sometimes she sang reveille:

> "You gotta get up
> You gotta get up
> You gotta get up
> In the morning!

>You gotta get up
>You gotta get up
>You gotta get
>Out o' bed!"

She stood in the doorway, already dressed for the day, in a shapeless pink homemade dress, with a Chesterfield in the same hand as her coffee cup and an ashtray in the other.

Dad was usually gone to the brewery by the time we came downstairs in the morning. All day he loaded tall brown bottles into wooden crates on a conveyor belt, or loaded passing cardboard cartons with cans. Some days he loaded the delivery trucks, a job he liked better because he could be outside.

"It's good for your muscles," he'd say. "Here. Feel that." And Bob and I would marvel at his big, hard biceps.

"Watch me make a muscle!" one of us would say, and both of us would flex our arms. Dad would pinch my biceps between his thumb and first knuckle and say, "You're getting strong!" and squeeze it till my knees buckled and I fell on the floor laughing, hurting, and rubbing my arm. And then he'd do the same to Bob.

He told us stories of bottles of beer that had come down the line with things inside: a rag, a cigar butt, a dead mouse. When either of us fetched him a beer, we were allowed the first swig, but we always held the bottle to the light first.

OUR HOUSE WAS a narrow brick row house painted with a thick cream enamel, and we had the last slate sidewalk on the block. The slate was broken and heaved up by the roots of a huge tree that shaded the front of the house. Dad called it "that god-damned hemlock," because the roots were cracking the walls of the storm sewer in front of our house and threatening the foundation. He'd already had to call a plumber to pump water out of the cellar.

Bob and I knew right where the crack was because the concrete bunker underneath the sidewalk was what we called "our secret hiding place." The crack was just below the corrugated metal drainpipe, an echoing darkness wide enough for skinny kids to crawl in and to back out. It led from the vault to wherever we decided on a given day: the sea, the center of the earth, China.

We took turns crawling into the pipe: I remember reaching ahead with my hands, feeling my way as far in front of me as possible, worried that the horizontal pipe might suddenly turn vertical and I'd find myself falling, plummeting toward the answer to our arguments.

"I think I heard the ocean!" I'd say to Bob as I backed out of the pipe. Or I'd tell him I saw a pair of glowing eyes in there. I was just as afraid whether I was in the cramped dark tube or waiting in the vault. A year older than Bob, I felt responsible for him. And of course each of us, once out of view, tried to scare the other by keeping silent.

WE'RE GOING ON a trip: Mom, Dad, baby Joey, Mammy Etta, Bob, and me. We're in a big, round, shiny black '50 Pontiac, my dad's first car. Joey's on Mom's lap; Bob, me, and Mammy are in the back. Bob and I want to sit next to each other, so we can fight, Mammy says. She lets us.

Lancaster is two hours from Allentown, four hours to look at things and places out the window! We look and fight till Dad says, "Etta, what the hell is going on back there?" We stop for gas; get back in the car with Mammy between us.

Bob cried all the way home, a bandage wrapped around his right leg, Mammy Etta's arms around him. I looked out the window, trying to get excited about the hills, the farms, the cows, the other cars, the billboards. Except for Bob, I don't remember anyone, all the way home, making a sound.

They'd done a biopsy, slit the back of Bob's right calf and snipped a bit of muscle from it. Minor surgery: to a child there's nothing more terrifying—the needle itself is terror, then a stranger, a grown-up, cuts you! My father decided to remove the sutures himself, a week or so later. Mom and I held Bob on the bed; Dad, with his tweezers, kept saying, "Keep still, damn it," while Bob screamed and cried. It must have been too early for the stitches to come out, because he bled; he had a tender, raised scar on his leg after that.

IT ALWAYS TOOK us a while to quiet down at bedtime, and my parents were always shushing us and telling us not to wake our baby brother, Joey, who slept in the crib in my parents' bedroom. Sometimes we stayed up playing chestnut football. On the embossed linoleum floor, a purple and pink floral design, patterned after an Oriental carpet, horse chestnuts were arranged in rows. The object of the game was to roll your running back, your roundest chestnut, down a cardboard ramp, and through eleven squat defenders, flat-sided chestnuts that had to be at least four fingers apart, without touching any of them. The further object of the game was to stay up as late as possible having fun, but without making enough noise to anger Dad and bring him upstairs.

In autumn we collected the chestnuts from around the neighborhood, prying them from their spiky cases and polishing them on our sweaters. Dad, inventor of chestnut football, told us they were called horse chestnuts because, like "horse corn," they were fit only for horses to eat, while another kind of chestnut, the kind that Nat King Cole sang about at Christmas, was delicious roasted. Horse chestnuts, Dad told us, were poison. Bob and I, daring each other, ate a little piece of one, and although it tasted awful, like a bad pistachio, and dried out your mouth like a crab apple, neither of us got sick from it.

Other times we knelt together at the floor register, a grate that allowed heat to rise from downstairs, and listened to the television and to our parents talking. Sometimes they argued, often about money.

"All I know's my mother raised the five of us on *half* of what you spend," Dad said. "I'm bustin' my ass, pulling double shifts, and, what the hell, look at this god-damn TV set. The picture tube's going; then what? I got a piece of linoleum plugging the hole in my shoe. We're eating Spam, for Christ's sake."

"You said you liked Spam."

"When I was in the Army, I said. I liked it when I was in the Army. Jesus, Dolly, we ain't got a pot to piss in!"

"So let me go to work! I could help with lunch at the high school. My mom said she'd watch the kids."

"No, god damn it, I said no. Wait. What's that? Is that those sneaky kids again?"

We dove back into bed and lay there, trying not to make a sound. After a while, we looked at each other, pulled imaginary zippers across our mouths, and crept back to the grate.

My mother stayed home; my father went out. It seems incredible to me, the energy he had. At times he worked two jobs. One he still remembers with pride was laying track for a diesel roundhouse at Bethlehem Steel. For a time he worked in a brewery and then unloaded sacks of spices at a warehouse in the evenings. When he wasn't working in the evenings he was always doing something—coaching baseball in summer, refereeing basketball in winter—I went along, a batboy in summer, and in winter a lonely spectator at basketball games between teams I didn't know. He knew, the former promising left-handed pitcher from the Boys' Club, that Bob's illness was called Duchenne's muscular dystrophy, and that it was progressive and lethal. He ran up and down the court, blowing his whistle, pointing his finger, shouting. "Foul on number nineteen. Hacking. On the arm. Two shots." Sometimes people booed, and I sat behind the scorer flushed with anger and embarrassment.

My mother stayed home. And wanted a girl this time, a Catherine Marie; carrying Michael Steven, who never learned to walk.

chapter four

1956

When i was in the second grade, my mother took a part-time job in a silk mill a couple of blocks from St. Francis of Assisi School. My father didn't know about it. One of my mother's sisters was already working there, I think. Mammy Etta took care of Joey. Aunt Kitty, my father's sister, was in on the secret too, along with Francie and Willy, who owned the greenhouse where my aunt worked. Instead of going home for lunch, Bob and I walked the three blocks to the greenhouse, where my aunt fed us, let us have the run of the place while she ate her own lunch, and made sure we left in time to get back to school.

We usually ate our lunch on a piece of oilcloth my aunt spread on the potting bench. She cooked us canned soup on a hot plate and let us drink tea with milk and sugar, which we never had at home. It was cool and damp in the potting shed, and the soup smells mingled with the raw sweet scent of soil and compost. We ate surrounded by towers of nested clay pots, under the eye of a sleepy old cat who seemed to find us too abrupt and energetic. It hissed at me once, and Aunt Kitty kicked it. (I remember this because it was the first time I ever heard a cat utter anything that actually sounded like meow.)

The potting shed, which faced the street, was also the shop, and a little bell jingled whenever someone came through the door. Above the cash register, a St. Francis calendar hung next to a clipboard, fat with orders, from which a pencil dangled on a piece of twine. In a row on the floor, shrubs waited for Willy to load on his truck. Wherever you looked there were plants and pots; brightly painted ceramic clowns, madonnas, burros, bluebirds, kittens; dirt-caked claws, hand spades, a pruner, shears.

After lunch we would jump down from the wobbly high stools and race through the doorway down three wooden steps into the greenhouse. It was steamy and warm, with light unlike any other, and the air seemed to shimmer, even in winter. Our response was pure, immediate, erotic, exhilarating. We couldn't help but run. The long tables along the clear glass walls (where here and there, for ventilation, a pane was propped open by a stick) were filled with flats of begonias, marigolds, violets, hyacinths, narcissus, lily of the valley, tulips, in various stages from sprout to blossom. Under the tables were watering cans and buckets, rakes and lengths of hose. Similar tables ran the length of the greenhouse in the center, with another aisle between them. For us it was a rectangular track with another corridor down the middle that made our play more interesting, keeping the pursuer guessing which way his quarry might turn. We chased each other around and around on the packed hard earth until Aunt Kitty yelled, "See here, you hooligans, it's time to get," and I don't remember Bob having any trouble yet. Sometimes I'd catch him and sometimes he'd catch me, and after some laughter and roughhousing the chase would start again in the opposite direction.

The secrecy surrounding my mother's job both disturbed and thrilled us. Bob's and my having lunch at the greenhouse once in a while required no explanation, but our going there every day was the little secret that would lead to the discovery of the big one, so we had to take care not to talk about it around my father. The women—my mother, Aunt Kitty, my mother's twin sisters, Marie and Marietta, and Mammy Etta—acted as if they were planning a surprise party. First they hugged and kissed us into complicity and then reinforced our sense of inclusion by winking. There was a lot of winking. Once, I remember, my father asked my mother where she'd been all day because he'd gone home and she wasn't there. Aunt Kitty was standing behind me, and she touched the back of my neck. It was just like a wink, and I knew I was supposed to be quiet.

"What the Sam Hill do you care what she does all day?" Aunt Kitty said, keeping her hand there. His big sister, she was the only one who could speak to my father this way.

"What's it to you? I was close by and I had a little time. Maybe I wanted to bring her a little present."

"Uh-huh. So where's this little present? I think you hoped she had a little present waiting for you!"

My father blushed and smiled and shook his head.

I looked at Bob. Both of us worried about what Dad might do if he found out, and we worried we wouldn't get to go to the greenhouse for lunch anymore.

SOMETIMES UNCLE FORREST helped Aunt Kitty at the greenhouse, especially around Easter and Mother's Day.

He loved to fish, and he loved to tell stories. In one of them he lost all his tackle to a fish so big that he tied a brightly colored shirt to his anchor, the fish swallowed it, and if his outboard engine hadn't run out of gas, he would have brought the monster to shore.

In the summer he gave us money for worms, a nickel a dozen, whenever he planned to go fishing. I always begged to go along and he always put me off by promising to take me when I got older. "I'm better at catching fish than catching worms," he said. "I leave that to the experts."

Dad didn't fish. "Hell, that's for guys who want to get away from their wives and drink beer, that's all. Your mother's not like that," he'd say, with a long pull on the tall brown bottle for emphasis.

"Besides, what kind of sport is that? A bunch of grown men sitting around on their fat asses waiting for some dumb fish to come along. They can't even see it. How would you like it? Think about it: you're minding your own business, not bothering anybody, and you go to take a bite out of your ice-cream cone and there's a hook in it and somebody pulls you right up out of your life, boom, just like that. What kind of sport is that?"

Nevertheless, at dusk my father would get out the hose and soak the grass in the backyard, and when it was dark and the yard had filled with lightning bugs, Bob and I would crawl on the grass, our coffee cans ready, while Dad clicked a flashlight on and off to locate the long night crawlers that would emerge partway from the earth and stretch themselves out in the wet grass. More than the merest flicker of light, or a clumsy move, would send the prey back in its hole. Too rough or too impatient and you tore the worm; not quick enough or indecisive and you lost it. Once you had hold of one, the thing to do was keep up a steady gentle pressure so the worm would slowly relinquish the fight and you could put it in your can untorn. Uncle Forrest was strict and half-worms didn't count.

THERE WAS ANOTHER secret. This must have been later, when I was in the third grade. My mother and Mammy Etta took Bob with them for the day, and at lunchtime I walked to the greenhouse alone. I was not to talk about the fact that Bob was anywhere but at school all day. My father was not to know. Uncle Webb, Mammy Etta's brother-in-law, was driving them to see a "powwow doctor," a Pennsylvania Dutch healer.

I had heard my grandmother saying something about it to my mother, and I thought she said they were going to take Bob to a "power doctor." He had begun falling down by then, mostly in the afternoon on the way home from school. He ran out of power too early in the day. It made sense to me.

"Are they going to fix Bob's power?" I asked Aunt Kitty.

"Phpht! Eat your noodle soup, and don't pay no attention to that there foolishness."

I was frightened, because Uncle Webb was driving. He had a wooden leg. I was under the kitchen table when I discovered it. His pants were hitched up, and he had on a real sock and shoe, but his leg was pink wood. I remember staring at it for a long time and thinking he should take a pencil and draw some curly hair on it so it would look more like the other leg. Did the power doctor cut off Uncle Webb's leg and give him a wooden one? Was that what he was going to do to Bob? I wanted to ask Aunt Kitty, but she was already upset by the whole thing; besides, I was worried that I was right.

"Does a power doctor give needles?"

"It's a 'powwow doctor.' And you don't need to know no more about it."

A powwow doctor had to be an Indian, I reasoned, and that scared me even more. The Indians were pagans and they had medicine men who fixed you up by painting different colors on you. The worst thing was that they prayed to false gods. It was a sin to go to them, like going to a church that wasn't Catholic. My mother, I knew, hadn't grown up Catholic, and Mammy Etta and Uncle Webb and everybody else in her family were Lutherans. It was a tension I was usually aware of as part of the confusing interactions of the two sides of my family, but now I felt it acutely. Aunt Kitty did not approve. My father was not to be told.

GROWING UP, I was puzzled and a little bothered by the strange symmetries and asymmetries of my family's names. For example, my mother's mother, Etta, was called Mammy, and my father's father, Edward, was called Pappy. At the same time, his wife, Elizabeth, was called Mommom.

We never met my mother's father, and it was not until many years later, after my mother's death, that I discovered that he and Mammy had never been married. Bob and I had always assumed that he'd been called away to something of the gravest importance. We thought of him as Peter or James or John, hauling in his net one day, minding his own business, when suddenly he's tapped on the shoulder. "Follow me." Frank Mattes was his name.

"What happened to your daddy?" one of us asked Mom.

"Oh, he went away when I was still a baby."

To add to the confusion, my mother's stepfather was named Hoffman. My mother took every opportunity to remind us that, even though he signed our Christmas and birthday cards "Grandpa Kenny," he was *not* our grandfather. My father was just as careful to tell us again and again that he was a different Hoffman, not from the Hoffman family that he and Aunt Kitty and my uncles and grandparents were part of.

"I don't know what rock that guy crawled out from under," my father would say, sneering.

What's more, Mammy Etta kept the name Hoffman after she and Kenny divorced. Loving her, and knowing there were two kinds of Hoffmans, I was uneasy on those rare occasions when the two sides of the family came together. My mother's twin half-sisters, Marie and Marietta Hoffman, Kenny's daughters, were our favorite baby-sitters when Bob and I were little, and have always been part of our family life. There were other shadowy people, who came around infrequently, some of them Mammy's family, some of them Kenny's, who were treated civilly but without warmth.

My mother had another half-sister, Anita, who lived an hour away, in Reading. Her son, Marty, also had muscular dystrophy. For a while, before my parents understood the disease, they seemed to take this as evidence that Kenny had done something to cause it. Marty died in his teens, a couple of years after Bob. I saw him at a family gathering the year before his death. When Gene, his father, wheeled him into the room, I was stunned. He looked so much like

Bob that I felt behind me for a chair. I took a deep breath and blinked back tears.

The last time I saw Kenny was at a cousin's wedding reception many years ago at the local firehouse. I hadn't seen him for at least a decade. I was carrying a big pot of my mother's baked beans to the kitchen. My cousin and his bride hadn't arrived yet. The band was tuning up.

"There's Kenny Hoffman," I said. He was tapping a pitcher of beer.

"The hell I care," my mother said. "Come put those beans over here."

I walked over to greet him, and was struck by his ratty mismatched jacket and baggy pants. His tie was stained. I put out my hand, but he had a mug in one hand and a pitcher in the other.

"Grandpa Kenny!"

"Yeah. Yeah. Hi. How are ya?" he said.

"Fine. I hope I get a chance to talk to you later on. It's been a long time." I meant it.

"Oh, hell, you know me," he said. "A half an hour and I'll be layin' drunk out in the gutter, and an hour after that I'll be in jail." He walked away.

Some of the discord between the two sides of my family came from the time of my parents' courtship, when, according to my father, much of their time together was spent baby-sitting my mother's sisters.

"Etta and Kenny. Those two. Hah. They were off in some god-damn barroom every night. Your mother raised those girls. She was the one made sure they ate and had clean clothes to wear. Not those two shitbirds. Agh! I shouldn't talk like that. Etta was fine once she got rid of that son of a bitch."

When he told me this, I felt as if I already knew it, and of course I did, and had, ever since I was very young, in the wordless way a child knows things like that.

I WENT DOWN the three steps into the greenhouse. Willy was carrying a large tray of some kind of seedlings down the middle aisle.

"Now don't you get it in your head one god-damn minute you can come in here and race around like monkeys. Go on. Back in the shop. I don't need no little dickens like you in my way. Go on!"

I turned to go. Aunt Kitty was in the doorway to the shop.

"Now wait a minute, Willy," she said. "He's a great big boy with lots of muscles. Maybe he can help. He's all by himself today."

"Well, them there begonias burnt all up. God damn it, I told Francie she had ought to have moved them. They need to go to the lath-house."

"We'll take care of it."

We loaded the trays of young plants on a big wooden cart and took them to the back of the greenhouse, where there was a little wooden shelter with a roof of crisscrossed strips of wood that let in a checkerboard of sunlight.

"This here's the hospital," Aunt Kitty said. "You see these here? Got too much sun. You see? You leave them out there and they drink up so much sunshine they get sick. Just like you kids and your candy bars and soda pop. They do all right in here though, if you catch them in time and doctor them back up."

Maybe there was a place like this for Bob. Maybe they could doctor him back up.

When I got home from school, Mom and Mammy Etta and Uncle Webb were sitting around the kitchen table drinking beer and smoking and eating pretzels from a bowl in the center of the table. No one was talking. Bob was upstairs in our room.

"It was dumb," Bob said. "They were talking all Dutchy and everything." He looked okay. They hadn't done anything to him that I could see.

"What did the doctor do? Was he an Indian?"

"He wasn't a doctor. He wasn't even dressed right. It was dumb. He wants me to wear a bag of stupid Dutchy words around my neck, and Mom says I have to, but I told her she can't make me."

"Maybe it could help you to not fall down so much."

"It's dumb! It's dumb! It's dumb!" He threw himself on the bed and cried.

Later, after Mammy Etta and Uncle Webb left, I asked my mother if I could see the bag with the writing in it.

"Never you mind about that bag," she said sternly. Then she changed her tone. "I'll show you later."

My father came in the front door.

"Just what the hell is going on around here is what I'd like to know."

My mother gave me a look that was more than a wink. I started back upstairs, listening.

"What do you mean?"

"They're digging up the whole god-damn street. There's PP&L trucks up and down the whole block. What the hell are they doing?"

"Oh. Well, how should I know? Should I call and find out?"

"Agh! Bring me a beer. How are the boys?"

Later my mother let me hold the powwow doctor's charm, a muslin pouch no bigger than a tea bag, tied at the top with a red string. She said there were German words inside but no one could read them because they were all torn up in little pieces, and if anybody opened the bag then the words wouldn't work. She took it from me, dropped it in her purse, and lit a cigarette.

"Will it help Bob to not fall down so much?"

My mother blew a great cloud of smoke.

"Who knows?" she said. She clicked her purse shut. "Nobody can say it won't."

chapter five

1957

AT ST. FRANCIS we learned about the Jordan River. On the other side was the Promised Land. Jesus was baptized there. When I was eight, I believed I'd seen the Jordan, that the fields and wooded hills on the other side of Jordan Creek were the Promised Land. I was afraid to go there because heaven and the Promised Land were confused in my mind, and if someone went to heaven, as Mommom had earlier that year, they did not come back. Along part of the creek, in summer, I could look across and see the superheated air boiling in ripples over a meadow yellow and purple with goldenrod and thistle. I'd never seen that anywhere else and believed I was glimpsing all you could see of the angels who would be visible if you crossed to the other side, the angels who were stirring the air with their wings.

Two hours a week were set aside for art. When we weren't studying the black-and-white reproductions in our art books, we were decorating the classroom along seasonal themes: turkeys, snowmen, Easter eggs. One of my classmate's parents had a turkey farm and they offered to bring a live turkey to school one day, but the nuns didn't think it was a good idea. Instead, we cut brightly colored construction paper into feathers and attached them to Styrofoam balls. The turkeys' heads were made of paper cups. At Christmastime we made countless pictures of snow and snowmen by applying a thick layer of blue crayon to a piece of cloth and then wiping it across our pencilled snowmen and snowdrifts to shade them in a way that, in fact, changed how I experienced real snow.

I liked to draw. Superman, Jesus, and Mickey Mantle were my subjects again and again. My mother was always effusive in her praise; my father could always spot a tracing. "Hell, anybody can *trace* a picture," he'd say. I couldn't understand how he could tell, every time. I tried to make a drawing so realistic he would mistake it for a tracing. Then I could challenge him to find the original.

In school, when we took out our art books, we got to see what heaven looked like. Some days we had color slides of paintings by Michelangelo, Fra Angelico, Leonardo. These were accompanied by scratchy records that beeped when it was time to press the red button to go to the next slide. Each depicted an event: the creation, the fall of Lucifer, the banishing of Adam and Eve from Paradise, the resurrection of Jesus, the assumption of Mary. One of my classmates asked if there were any photographs of Jesus. After explaining that the camera hadn't been invented yet, the nun turned the subject to the shroud of Turin, which was a kind of "miraculous photograph," much like Veronica's veil, which held the likeness of Jesus' face but had since been lost, captured, or destroyed, like the Holy Grail, by heathens. She passed around a book with a brown photograph of the shroud, and I saw that it was true: Jesus did have that distinctive double-pointed beard he had in the books and in the stained-glass windows of the church. Some of the painters had gotten the contours of his face wrong, however; it was long and square like a shoebox. Of course, it was further explained to us that the "miraculous photograph" was not really of Jesus, but only of his dead body, which he would reclaim on Easter morning. I never doubted any of it. The pictures ratified the stories, and the stories, read in church and cited and recited every day in school, confirmed the pictures; therefore, it was all true.

More than incense, music, Latin, candles, and robes, for a child the Catholic Church is the human figure, again and again, the body's beautiful proportions, the shadowed declivities of ankles crosshatched on the stained glass, the statues almost calling out to be touched, the veins in the hands almost pulsing. The men, all of them, luxuriantly bearded, rugged, and serene.

Jesus' hands in cryptic gesture. Joseph holding lilies or tools. Peter, the one with the keys.

And Francis, Francis of Assisi, his hands and feet mutilated with the stigmata, eyes closed in ecstasy beneath his smooth brow and bony crown, his beautiful, strong-looking, too-big feet in sandals. The public-school kids called him St. Francis the Sissy.

In his studio, Mr. Neff was working on his stained-glass window of St. Francis for the new church. He invited Bob and me inside on our way to school. There were racks of colored glass, a set of stairs that moved on a short length of track in front of a wall of white fluorescent light. There were long flat drawers he pulled out to show us his drawings, and a rack for what he called cartoons. They were watercolors, really, that would be translated into glass, piece by colored piece. In back, his assistant, wearing a visored helmet, moved around, taking no notice of us, welding things with an acetylene torch. Mr. Neff put his huge hand on my head and gave it a twist that brought my body around to face him.

"No, no," he said. "Don't either of you look at the torch. It'll hurt your eyes."

It was even more astonishing than church. This was the place where the glass was fired and colored and assembled to trick the sunlight into telling us the story we believed we were a part of. Although I couldn't fully grasp this, I could feel the power of the place. It was magic.

Bob and I passed the studio every day. Pieces of glass were arranged on shelves in all the windows. I wondered why Mr. Neff would choose to decorate the windows with odd-shaped pieces of blue, red, and yellow glass instead of a picture of a saint or the Good Shepherd or something like that. Bob said it would be a sin to do that, because only a church was allowed by God to have those kinds of pictures in the windows.

Any secular art we saw was bucolic, preindustrial: peasants in the fields, landscapes, horses pulling sleighs. The world of these reproductions was somehow more real to me than the world of sidewalks and traffic lights and snow that got down inside my galoshes and left my ankles red and raw.

THE SCHOOL HAD a triangular yellow SHELTER sign out front, and we had frequent air-raid drills, because, according to the nuns, the Russians were going to bomb us. Bob was in second grade; I was in third. We were afraid. We prayed to the Virgin Mary to stop them.

The sisters told us we need not fear death if we were good Catholics. From what they told us, Bob and I imagined that if the Russians killed us we would get up afterward the way we did when the bell rang while we were playing soldiers in the fields behind the school at recess. Then we would stand in line outside the door—of heaven, not school—to meet Jesus. We went to daily Mass and Tuesday-night novenas and tried hard to believe this.

We played war every chance we got. Sometimes it was just the two of us, so we drew blades of grass to see who would be the American. The other could choose to be a German, an Italian, a Japanese, a Korean, a Chinese, or a Russian. The game was modified hide-and-seek; the object was to sneak up undiscovered on the enemy, and kill him by making the most realistic rifle or machine-gun sounds you could. Sometimes we used dry clods of dirt for hand grenades, because they gave off a little puff of smokelike dust if you hit a rock or a tree with one. More often eight or ten of us from the neighborhood would play. If we played at recess, we used sticks for guns; if we played after school or in the summer, we had plastic rifles or tommyguns, helmets, Army-surplus belts, and canteens filled with Kool-Aid. Our Viewmasters, stereoscopes that otherwise brought us the Lone Ranger or Hopalong Cassidy in 3-D, became binoculars, hanging from our necks with scratchy twine.

The game began at opposite ends of the uncut meadow we called the prairie, which was soon filled with infantry crawling toward each other in the tall grass, snipers climbing trees, soldiers digging foxholes, voices imitating gunfire and explosions, and occasionally the sounds of a nasty argument. The rules of the game were unclear, and we had no referees, so much of the imaginary warfare took the shape of arguments as to who shot whom first, or how close you had to be to shoot someone. The worst thing you could do was refuse to die. "I had you!"

"No you didn't! I was covered! You can't shoot through a tank! I was behind this rock. This rock's a tank, man."

"Aw bullshit, man; you're dead." After that you were ignored, no matter what you did, and you had missed your chance to die dramatically, throwing your rifle in the air, crying out, staggering and tumbling to the ground, which was one of the best parts of the game.

MY FATHER USED to watch a program on Sunday nights called *Air Power,* narrated by Walter Cronkite, a documentary of all the major air battles and bombings of World War II. Bob and I watched it often. In jerky, too-fast footage, Allied pilots smiled from bomber cockpits and flashed the thumbs-up sign. A ground crew, in coveralls, laughed while painting a bomb. They stepped back: "Kilroy Was Here." Then the sky was filled with B-29s in formation. Cronkite's voice came over the drone of the bombers as the doors in the bellies of the planes opened. The bombs, looking like black fish, fell straight down, evenly spaced, whistling. Then we were seeing towns, and little puffs of smoke, like the ones our dry clods made, in orderly rows. After that the films showed burning buildings, people crying in the streets, and crews of men digging out trapped people and the bodies of the dead.

We became afraid of planes. We watched to see if the doors in their bellies would open, or if paratroopers would tumble from behind the wing. At night I often dreamed that Bob and I were roller-skating on the sidewalk when we heard the drone of a plane overhead; I looked up to see the trickle of bombs beginning to fall. We skated as fast as we could to the school, looking back over our shoulders and hearing the first explosions. When we got to the school, Sister Anne Catherine was in the doorway telling us to hurry. We tried to clatter up the steps in our skates but kept falling down. Bob was crying, and I tried to drag him up the steps. One time he woke me because I was calling his name in my sleep. I told him the dream, and we stayed awake the rest of the night and talked.

THE NUNS HAD given us comic books in school. Usually our comics were of Sergeant Rock battling the Japs or Nazis with a gun that said "Ratatatatatatatatat," but these showed a Catholic family in their fallout shelter saying the rosary together. We tried to get my father to build a fallout shelter and to say the rosary with us. We talked about what we would do if we survived the bombs. We agreed that we'd play possum so the enemy would think that we were dead. Sometimes in bed at night we would practice keeping still and holding our breath.

My parents had a world atlas, and in the back of it were color plates of the flags of all the countries of the world. We tore out those pages and stuck them up in the window of our bedroom. We weren't sure who the enemy was—the Germans or the Japanese or the Italians or the Koreans or the Chinese or, probably, the Russians—but the idea was that a pilot flying over Ninth Street would spot his flag on our window and not bomb our house.

THE NUNS AT school were sure Russia was the enemy. Russians hated Jesus, and they loved to torture people to test their faith. They would try to make us deny Jesus, like St. Peter. If we were caught alone, they would try to make us lead them to our families so they could kill them too.

Otto Schlemcher was my idea of a Russian. He was big—an eighth-grader—who bullied Bob and me almost daily. Dark and ugly, he walked with a sort of lurch and he mumbled; it was hard to make out what he said. We knew that the other eighth-graders laughed at him. Bob and I feared and hated him; we thought his name was as weird and ugly as he was.

It was that spring of 1957 that Bob began to weaken. Stairs gave him trouble. One day he fell on the way home from school. I was giving him a hand getting up, when Otto was suddenly there. He pushed me, and Bob went down again. "Leave us alone, you Commie," I said.

"What you call me?"

"You're a Commie Russian," Bob said. He'd gotten himself on all fours, and Otto grabbed him by the hair. "Take that back," he said and pulled.

Bob started crying. "I take it back, okay, I take it back."

Otto let go.

"Leave him alone," I said.

"What it to you, punk-face?" He came after me and got me in a headlock and rapped my head with his knuckles until I cried. When he let me go, I swung at him and hit him as high as I could reach, on the shoulder. "You can't even talk right," I yelled at him and ran across the street.

Bob tried to run. Otto caught him and knocked him down, hard, on a low picket fence that bordered someone's front yard. He shouted something across the street at me and lurched away.

Bob's shirt was torn and his back and ribs were scraped and bleeding. Dad called the Schlemchers while Mom painted Bob's ribs with Mercurochrome. He must have got Otto's father on the phone. He started yelling. "Don't give me that crap. That's no excuse. Next time I'll call the cops. Oh, yeah? You better hope I don't come over there, that's all I have to say." My mother called the school.

The next day Bob was absent from school, but Otto and I had to go to the principal's office and apologize to each other. There were four nuns in the room, looking sternly at us and slowly shaking their heads. After Sister Elizabeth Mary told Otto he could leave, they all sat down and explained to me that I should *never* make fun of Otto again, because he couldn't help the way he walked and slurred his words. He had a terrible disease called palsy.

chapter six
1958

THE YEAR I turned nine, Bob was fitted with brown leather braces to wear at night. Dad always laced them too tightly, and Bob would cry out that they pinched him. "They won't work, damn it, if they're not on tight!" Dad would scold him. There was going to be a cure, a rescue, if we could only hang on. But if Bob allowed the tendons in his calves to tighten up, the cure, when it came, would be too late. So Dad tied the rawhide laces tight and Bob did his best not to complain. We lay in our bed in the dark.

"The left one hurts."

"Go to sleep."

"It's killing me. It's pinching. Can you fix it?"

"It has to be on tight or it won't work."

"Just pull it away from the skin where it pinches."

I could just get my index finger under the leather collar that choked Bob's calf; by working it around, I could free the skin that had been caught. Often the collar was too tight to get my finger under it.

"Fix it!"

"I can't. Shut up and go to sleep."

"I can't."

"Well, just shut up till Dad gets back."

This was the routine: after half an hour Dad would climb the stairs to feel Bob's toes. If they were cold, he turned on the light to look at them; if they were blue, he loosened the laces.

Not long after that, Bob slammed my shin with one of the heavy braces and I knocked him out of bed. Mom and Dad came running. Dad straddled me on the bed and grabbed me by the front of my pajamas. "Selfish," he called me. A smack in the face. And "lucky." Smack. I was a "bully." He was going to teach me. Smack. My mother stopped him. Bob was crying on the floor. Dad picked him up and put him back in the bed, where I lay with my face turned to the wall.

Another night or two and Bob was sleeping on a cot in the middle room downstairs. Soon our toys and games were divided between what was now my room and a tall metal wardrobe next to the cot downstairs. I was alone. I kept the crystal radio that Dad had helped us assemble from a kit when we had the chicken pox. I kept the Swiss Army knife we used to saw flashlight batteries in half. The reason they didn't work, Dad said, was they were out of juice. Whenever a battery didn't work, we cut it open. Dad was right. No juice in it. We never cut open a battery that still worked; that would have been stupid. Besides, if we cut one open that still had juice in it, we were sure Dad wouldn't buy another one. We believed he knew how long a battery should last, how much juice it had, and how long it took to dry up. "Batteries don't grow on trees," he said.

I don't think I knew then, at least not in a way I understood, how much I missed Bob, especially at bedtime. After all, he was still around, still there to fight with at the breakfast table, still there to play Parcheesi on the floor, still my brother.

At bedtime, in the dark, the street lamp outside cast the shadow of a tree limb on the ceiling. When it moved in the breeze, heaving and fluttering, I thought I could feel the bed shake. The quivering leaf shadows were a mob of winking gnomes. The objects in the room changed into animals; even the folds of the sheets could turn into menacing presences. I seemed to hear the world outside for the first time—cars, doors slamming, the screech and thud of distant trains coupling in the railroad yard, voices too far off to understand. Each sound had to do with me, and each was a warning. Whatever it was that snuck up on Bob unnoticed might be trying to get me too.

Soon after that I began to have a recurring nightmare that was all the more terrifying because it took place in my bedroom. I was standing in front of the mirror that was mounted on the dresser at the foot of my bed. I tried not to look at my eyes in the mirror; whenever I did, a cackling, high-pitched laugh began and from behind the mirror came first the white-gloved knuckles of two hands, and then the head of a clown, an animated puppet who paused with his nose between his hands like those "Kilroy Was Here" cartoons from World War II. The fevered laughing got louder as the clown's head rose above the mirror and sneered at me. I began screaming, in the dream, and woke sitting up in my bed. At the foot of the bed was the dresser and mirror. Then I screamed for real, until my parents rushed into my room. More than once my father tried to convince me that there was no room for such a clown in the inch or two behind the mirror, but it didn't matter. I insisted that there was a bad clown behind the mirror. I never thought to ask that the dresser be moved or the mirror taken down. I dreaded going to bed at night. I begged my parents to let me sleep with them.

My mother gave me a rosary that glowed in the dark. When I asked her how it held the light, she said she didn't know. "Is it special blessed?" I asked her.

"I'm sure it's blessed. I bought it at the Altar and Rosary Society breakfast. It works best if you shine a light on it every once in a while."

So every night I took the rosary from my bedpost and coiled it under the lamp next to my bed while I put on my pajamas and said my prayers. "... if I should die before I wake, I pray the Lord my soul to take." Then I called down blessings on each of my parents, my baby brother Mike, Joey, Bob, and every member of my family I could remember. My fear of being left in the dark alone was an aid to memory as one name called up another and another all the way down to my mother's second cousins on her stepfather's side. When I ran out of names, I offered my prayers up for a "special intention," as the nuns at St. Francis called it, the same one every night. "And may Bob get better soon. Amen." Then I got under the covers, gathered the coiled rosary in my palm, and turned off the lamp. As I thumbed the beads, blessed again with light, I drifted into a trance induced by the rhythm and sibilance—"pray for us sinners"—of my own voice whispering in the darkness—"now and at the hour of our death. Amen."

At St. Francis we learned about the souls in purgatory and that we could help them get to heaven by suffering and offering it up for them. They in turn would remember us when they ascended to heaven and would intercede for us. I offered up my prayers and my penance for Mommom, who was the only person I knew who had died. I was convinced she didn't really need my help. My father said he was sure she had gone straight to heaven because she was so good. Still, I took to folding my legs back under me in a painful way, and I tried to withstand the pain a little longer each night, counting how many decades of the rosary I recited before I had to give up and unbend my legs. Gradually I became less afraid. The rosary's incantatory power brought a kind of peace to me; after a while the cyclical sounds were released from their meanings, and I was released from my yearning—for my brother and for things to return to normal—and I slept.

In a comic book I read about telepathy, and I showed it to Bob. I don't remember if it was my idea or his, but we tried it for a while, long enough to arrive at some rules. The trouble was that we fought all the time, because we each believed that if the other would only quit *sending* so much and spend more time trying to *receive,* it would work. I remember one time when I convinced myself that he had agreed to give me his Warren Spahn and Eddie Matthews baseball cards. He denied it. I took the cards, but my mother made me give them back. We decided to start out more simply. We each kept a tablet and pencil next to our beds to write down what we wanted to send as well as anything we thought we had received. In the morning we would compare our pages. We never matched, so we decided to try to send single words. As we tired of the whole thing, we each began to write long lists of all the words that occurred to us once we were in our separate beds. Every morning we would find that some of our words matched, just enough of them for us to believe, with each other's help, that we were getting somewhere. After a while we gave up.

I believed that Bob was the problem, though I knew it wasn't his fault. Maybe it was part of his illness, like falling down all the time.

So I lay in bed and tried to contact aliens: Martians or Venusians. This was similar to praying, except that, while I took it for granted that God heard me, I wasn't sure if any aliens were listening, or if I had telepathic powers strong enough to reach them. There was no formula that I knew of for communicating with aliens, no Hail Mary's or Glory Be's. This hit-or-miss dimension made it even more exciting. And then there was the element of listening; though God sometimes spoke to people, they were almost always grown-ups. In any case, I didn't expect a reply from God. I would know, however, that the aliens had "heard" me only if they answered. I don't know what I expected, maybe something like, "Check. We read you, earth boy. We are standing by."

I remember that Bob was alarmed when I let on what I was up to. How would I know if they were friendly aliens? What if they sent me a whole brainful of scary thoughts? What if they tried to take over my mind?

What I thought but never told him—and this, I suspect, I got from a *Twilight Zone* episode on TV—was that the alien I was trying to contact was a superior intelligence, probably with a huge head like a light bulb, who would give me the cure for whatever had made him sick. I kept the tablet and pencil next to the bed. I imagined the cure would be too complicated for me to grasp, but that the alien would send me the message slowly so I could write it down and give it to scientists who would understand it. On the other hand, the cure might be something simple, something we were overlooking, and the alien would point it out, and I would tell my mother the next morning and everything would be okay.

I knew that Bob's sleeping downstairs was permanent, but it was the kind of knowledge I wouldn't, or couldn't, surrender to. With so much changing so fast, how could I believe anything was "for keeps," as we called it? There were braces, there were prayers, there was telepathy, and there was hope.

In a few more months the school year would be over. By the end of that summer, Bob was in a wheelchair. In September he was going to a different school.

chapter seven

1959

THE TWO LOCAL breweries, Neuweiler's and Horlacher's, where my father worked, were next to Riverfront Park; there Tom Feifel coached the Downtown Youth Center Bears 110-pound football team. Just across the Lehigh River was the Arbogast and Bastian slaughterhouse and meat-packing plant, its symbol two interlocking hearts with an arrow through them, like something a romantic kid would carve on a tree. There were times, especially in late summer, when practice began, that the smell of the hops and sweet barley malt from the breweries combined with the stench of slain pigs and steers to overpower us, and we begged Tom to cancel practice.

"What are you, pussies?" he would jeer at us. "Line up for calisthenics!" Often somebody would throw up, and, led by Tom, we would all join in the ridicule. "Hey, wussy," Tom would yell at the gagging kid, "if you feel something hairy coming up swallow quick 'cause it's your asshole!"

"Get mad!" he would shriek, red in the face. "Get mad!" Two of us would hold the blocking dummies, bracing them with all our weight, in order to leave a passage between them wide enough only for one. The two combatants, competing for a spot in the starting lineup faced each other on all fours in the dirt.

"Ready. On the whistle."

At the whistle's short blast, we would lunge for the opening, butting our helmeted heads together like goats.

The whistle again, to stop.

"You call that hitting? That was a god-damned love tap! Hit him for Christ's sake. You go over that man, you hear? I want to see him on his back. I want to see your footprints on his chest. Get mad! You want to play on Sunday? Do you? Then show me, damn it!"

It was all right to cry, as long as you cried with gritted teeth and lips curled back, roaring, snot or even blood running from your nose, as long as your crying was accompanied by rage, as long as you thirsted for victory.

We easily won the championship. The other teams were mostly ragtag groups of kids with someone's father for coach. We were considered better disciplined, better schooled in the fundamentals, better coached. The other kids were scared of us.

I still have the team picture from the newspaper, yellowed and coming apart where it's folded. Tom's not in it.

SCOOTER WAS A halfback, skinny and quick. I liked to pair off with him for drills, since he couldn't hit very hard. I got to know him because Tom used to pick me up in his station wagon for practice, and Scooter was usually with him, riding shotgun. He was a grade ahead of me at St. Francis.

One fall day he asked me if I wanted to see something

neat after school, and we went to a spot called the fort in the field behind the school called the prairie. Weathered boards and a piece of oilcloth covered a shallow bunker dug into a hill, and the approach was guarded by a thorny patch of wild raspberries, white wands of stickers that were hard to wade through. Unless you were wearing crisp new jeans or a long coat, you had to pick your way through, moving one prickly whiplike branch at a time. When we were playing army, the fort was virtually invulnerable to surprise attack.

My hands were cold, so it must have been at least November. I didn't have gloves on. As I worked my way through the raspberry brambles to the fort, Scooter fired a match rocket at me. We used to buy stove matches, Ohio Blue Tips that you could scratch on anything to light, and by first wetting the tip on your tongue, you could snap it into flame on your thumbnail and in one motion shoot it in an arc that left a smoke trail behind it. By the time I got through the tangled raspberry wands, I'd had to slap one burning match from my shoulder and stamp on another where it had landed in the long dry grass.

"You want to start a fire?" I yelled. "Be careful."

I knelt next to Scooter with my hands in my pockets. My toes were cold in my torn sneakers.

"Look," he said, and he held up a mouse by its tail. The little creature pawed the air and twisted this way and that.

"Here. Hold him. Don't let him get away."

I pinched its tail and held the mouse up in front of my face, studying its black eyes, pink nose, yellow teeth. It squirmed and twisted, and it was all I could do to keep hold of it.

"Here. Put him in here."

I tried to lower the mouse into a coffee can he'd lined with dry grass, but it kept arching its back and grabbing onto the edge of the can with its hairless paws. After two or three tries, I closed my other hand around the animal and got it in the can.

The mouse tried to leap out, fell back on the dry grass, and spun around and around on his hind legs scratching at the smooth metal.

Scooter struck the match off his front tooth, and it hissed into flame. What he intended did not occur to me until he dropped it in the can.

The mouse screamed and flailed upward as the flames took it. I remember the smell of burning fur and the splayed pink paws like tiny hands. I remember the moment when it fell backward and blistered in the flames.

I couldn't speak. I couldn't even look at Scooter. All I could do was stand and then, with my hands deep in my jacket pockets, wade through the crisscrossed thorns that tore at my thighs through my pants.

Scooter shouted after me, "You did it too! We did it together! Both of us! You did it too!"

MY FATHER IS the coach, and I am the batboy, of the Herbert Paul Lentz Post #29 American Legion baseball team. I'm in my uniform, a smaller version of his, although I'm bothered that I don't have pants like his, with the black-and-gold braid down the side, only baggy gray ones. We're early, there to line the base paths, batter's box, coach's boxes, and on-deck circles. None of the teenage players have arrived yet.

"Go limp. Like a puppet. You'll never get hurt that way. Hit, crumple, and roll. Okay, ready? Stand up. And hook up."

These are jumpmasters' commands, and I mime obedience, standing and reaching up to lock my clip on the static line that will pull the chute from my pack when I have plummeted some distance from the plane. When I jump I yell, "Geronimo!" My sneakers hit the grass and I let my knees buckle, dip my shoulder, land on thigh, hip, shoulder, and roll over and over in the lush summer grass. When I look up, my father smiles and flashes me the thumbs-up sign.

I remember he tried to teach this skill to Bob too, when his falls were getting more dangerous; he would hit the ground with his knees first, then whiplash forward without the strength in his arms to break his fall. Often his face was black and blue and scabby. Dad and I both tried to get him to tuck his shoulder and roll when his legs buckled, but Bob never mastered it. I remember being proud of being able to jump from higher and higher places without getting hurt.

The growing distance between Bob and me was partly my need to believe that he could learn, if only he would try a little harder, how not to get hurt. I wanted him to practice with me. "Let's go outside and play paratrooper," I'd say, but he never felt like it. I knew he was sick, but I needed to hold him responsible for at least some part of it. If my brother's disease could slam him into the ground at any moment, bloodying his nose and blacking his eyes, there was no hope. If he were completely helpless, I would have to feel it: not only the sidewalk smashing him in the face, but also his outrage and humiliation, and, worst of all, my grief. No. Not my brother. He's too smart. He could get the hang of it if he would try.

I loved riding next to Dad in the car, his dusty spikes on the floor in front of me while he drove in his stirruped stocking feet. "Nobody in the valley knows baseball better than your dad," the father of one of his players said. "They say that he's a bird dog for the Reds; is that true?" I didn't know; besides, I didn't know for sure if a bird dog was a good thing or not.

"Oh, hell," Dad said when I asked him, "anybody can be a bird dog. All you have to do is know a few scouts. A bird dog's a guy who watches a lot of kids play ball and when he sees somebody who might be major-league material he calls up one of the scouts. If the scout likes the kid and signs him to play, the bird dog gets a few bucks. You just have to know who the scouts are. There might be a guy around to look at a couple of the kids this week or next. I know him, but these guys don't want the whole world to know who they are, so I don't say nothing. People can figure it out for themselves. It don't make no difference anyway."

I watched for scouts, convinced I'd know one if I spotted him. I took a handful of safety pins from my mother's sewing box, turned my baggy gray pants inside out, and used the pins to take in the inside seam of both legs. A scout would never consider a guy with baseball pants so loose they flapped in the wind. The trouble was that the pins would sometimes come undone, and once, playing paratrooper off the topmost bleacher seat, I jammed a pin deep in the flesh of the inside of my thigh. When I pulled it out, I could feel blood running down my leg. I crawled on my elbows to the cover of a nearby shrub, pretending

I'd been shot. There was blood on my pants, and later, when one of the players asked me what had happened, I said I'd gotten spiked stealing second base.

In my fantasy, the scout, who looked like anybody else, walked up to my father after a game and, taking a Yankees cap from his pocket, slapped it on his thigh, tugged it on, spit, and said, "The batboy. We could use that kid. He's major-league material."

I WAS IN the back seat of Coach Tom's car, in the parking lot of an ice-cream, pizza, and sandwich shop on Seventh Street, just beyond the bridge where, ten years old that year, I caught my first two fish. The first was a fat spring sucker I netted as it shimmied up the icy, ankle-deep white rapids just west of Seventh Street to spawn in calmer water. My feet numb, I waded ashore with my prize, a pulsing muscle squirming in my hands, my blood pounding. I remember the shame when the thrashing changed to a shudder, and my wonder when, after I thought it was dead, it slapped the bank once more with its tail.

The other was my first trout, caught exactly the right way too, on a tiny size 20 hook slipped under the metallic green collar of a Japanese beetle from a shrub beside the water. I saw the whole thing. The beetle floated over him, glinting like a jewel, its shadow moving along the gravel bottom, and the trout turned, moved downstream, turned again, and waited for it like a confident outfielder under a pop-up. Up, a sip, a flick of the tail, the lazy return to his station. My ears were hot and pounding. My hands shook. I took in the slack and pulled. I had him!

I felt the same pounding that day in the parking lot after baseball practice. The same shaking hands. Tom has pulled into the shade of the mint-green cinder-block building, neon beer signs in the windows, the *dink-dink-whack* of pinball machines. One by one I am holding color slides up to the light, slides of grown-ups doing amazing things, astonishing things. I am trembling, and my fingers fail. I drop a slide.

Tom cuffs me on the side of my head above my hot red ear. "All right, that's it, no more for you. I told you to be careful."

My blood's at flood tide. Induced, premature, with a hunger urgent as an infant's, my sexuality is born, a beggar. "No, please. I'm sorry. I'll be careful. Honest."

"Let's get some ice cream, shithead."

"But wait. I want . . ."

But the slides are back in the yellow cardboard sleeve and he is locking it away in the glove box. Later I will learn from him how people relieve this painful wanting, but for now I can only cry, hiding my face in my arms, leaning on the front seat. My new baseball glove is on the floor between my feet.

"You fuckin' crybaby. Stay here." The door slams but I don't look up. Soon he's back.

"Here. Eat it, damn it, before it melts."

TOM'S HOUSE, WHERE he lived with his mother, was near the bottom of the steep Sixth Street hill, just across from the entrance to the park. The street was closed off in winter. Kids with sleds flashed down the hill. Others, on broken cardboard cartons from the nearby bakery, spun round and round, laughing but envious of those who ran and flopped and shot past in a straight fast run downhill. The row of houses on the west side of the street descended, of necessity, more gradually than the hill itself, so that the farther down the hill you went, the more steps there were up to the front doors of the houses. It was two whole flights of concrete steps to Tom's front door.

Tom slapped my ass as he got up and pulled up his pants. "Go take a shit," he said, nodding toward the bathroom.

The bathroom was powder blue with gold flecks in it. Furry, fluffy rugs and toilet-seat cover and a doll with crotcheted skirt demurely camouflaging the spare roll on top of the tank.

I sat and tried to reason. Something was wrong with me. This was supposed to be fun. "Come on, let's have some fun," Tom would say on the way to his house. He kept his slides and 8mm movies in the bedroom there, and while he threaded the film or loaded the slide projector, he would let me look at cartoon books of Donald and Daisy Duck, Popeye and Olive Oyl, Mickey and Minnie Mouse doing the same things the people in the slides and movies were doing.

Then the projector would start clicking and a white square of light would appear and turn into colors that Tom would focus to writhing, sweat-glistened bodies. There was no sound but the whirring of the projector and Tom's occasional grunting. Reaching around from behind me, he would take my penis between his thumb and forefinger, saying, "You like this, don't you? You like this, don't you?"

Sometimes I did feel giddy and out of control, but right then I felt vaguely sick to my stomach, not as if I'd eaten something rancid, but fluttery and strange. Either the force of his penetration was reverberating in my system, or I was learning, as I sat there trying to make sense of what was happening, how to keep myself from crying, from even knowing I felt hurt. Probably both. I shit, and turned around to look, having never seen sperm. I'd been told by my father that it was a seed. I knew from the slides that it was a kind of jelly, and I thought that a seed must be suspended in it like the seeds in a grape. So I looked for a seed. I didn't see any.

By the time I came out of the bathroom, I thought I had figured out what was wrong. Tom was in the living room, drinking beer and watching a ball game. I put a smile on my face and a bounce in my walk and said, as casually as I could, "Next time we should try it the other way around, and I'll do that to you."

He laughed, then put his hand on my chest and pushed so that I staggered backward across the room and into the sofa. "Sit down and shut up," he said.

I wanted to cry but I didn't dare. I bent over with my arms folded across my belly, pretending to watch the ball game. Mostly I felt ashamed for being so stupid. Why was I unable to understand what was going on? The more I learned, the more confused and ashamed I became. I knew lots of things the other kids didn't. I knew that Minnie Mouse liked to have Mickey lick her pussy, loudly: Slurp, slurp!, the caption read. I knew that Popeye's prick was as big as his arm, that Olive Oyl could nevertheless take all of it inside her, smiling, and that Bluto's, by contrast, was laughably small, which was why he was such a bully. I knew that even more astonishing than the union of man and woman was the so-called gang-bang. I knew that Coach Tom's penis was uncircumcised, although I didn't know how to name that difference then. I knew that sex was sinister, clandestine, hot, and universal. I may have even known that my childhood was over.

ONE DAY, COMING home from Tom's house, I was walking in the front door when I heard a crash. My father was yelling, "Damn it Jesus fuckin' Christ!" and Bob was screaming. I ran into the room and found Dad on the floor, swearing, pounding his fist on the carpet, teeth gritted, unable to move. Bob had fallen in the corner, partway up the wall, his neck bent at a grotesque angle. I froze looking down at my father. "Help your brother, you asshole!"

Mom came running down the stairs. "What happened?"

"Call the doctor!" I shouted. Mike was shrieking in the next room. The doorbell rang—our next-door neighbor. My father said, "You don't let anybody in here, damn it. You'll be sorry." I didn't. I said that some shelves had fallen. "Thanks, but everything's all right." The doctor came: Bob was unhurt, a nosebleed and a bump on the head; my father had ruptured a disc in his back.

MY FATHER HAD always been given to sudden rages, even when we were little. Some days he came home from work already angry about something, and we were careful not to provoke him. Some days that was impossible, and he would pull his belt from his trousers, double it, and come after us. "I'll teach you!" he'd shout.

Now I had become the target for his rage. He would chase me, and I would try to keep some piece of furniture between us: the kitchen table, or the sofa, or Bob in his wheelchair. Sometimes he would corner me and, as he kicked at me, huddled on the floor, he'd shout, "Get up! Get up off the god-damned floor!"

It must have seemed to him that life was sneering at his every plan. It wasn't me he wanted to "get up off the god-damned floor." He must have been living in hell.

How many times did I walk out, careful not to slam the door and further enrage him? Out into the yard with its robins and squirrels, slugs and salamanders, the little bugs that rolled up into tiny armadillos, the praying mantises my mother called clothespin bugs. How many hypnotic hours did I throw a ball, hard, at the strike zone chalked on the shed? Beyond the yard was the neighborhood; beyond the neighborhood, the town. I was learning how to leave.

Sometimes, trapped in a corner, I couldn't get away from him, and afterward, bringing my elbows down from beside my head and uncurling my hunkered body, I only knew I had been gone, not where. That was something else I was learning, another kind of leaving: when there was nowhere to go, that's where I went.

A CANVAS DUFFLE held the bats. The balls were in a bowling bag. We sat on the bench taking off our street shoes and putting on our molded rubber spikes. Curt, Pete, Angelo, Patrick, Scooter. We played catch and pepper, took infield and outfield practice, batting practice if it was a home game. When the game began, I took my position on the bench, second from the bats, next to Tom, who kept rolling a baseball in his hands, running his long yellow fingernails along the seams, hardly watching the game for minutes at a time, looking up and yelling something, angrily, once in a while, but mainly staring down at the ball in his hands, turning it this way and that, over and over. My father stood just behind the bench, his arms folded across his chest, or behind the backstop, bent at the waist, arms up, hanging on the chain link screen. "Let's hear some chatter out there!" he'd say. The guys on the field would answer.

"Hon you baby. Fire it in there. Hon you babe."

"No batter. No batter."

I understood I would not get into the game. There were a couple of other boys on the bench with me, but they weren't ballplayers, not real ones. They didn't care about the game the way I did. They didn't even know how to put on a uniform. My father had shown me the secret. After you had your white sanitary hose and baseball socks on, you turned your pants inside out, placed the elastic where you wanted it on your legs, rolled the now double socks down over the elastic band, stood, and pulled up your pants. That's the way real ballplayers wore their uniforms, not with the elastic showing or their socks falling down.

I always watched the game intently, even though I was certain I wouldn't play. I wanted to have plenty to say to my father on the way home. "How long are you gonna sit there getting splinters in your ass?" he always asked, but he needed someone to talk with about the game, and if I paid perfect attention to the way it had unfolded, I could learn from him what the turning points had been and what might have made a difference. By the time we arrived home, we had shared the game, and it didn't seem to matter as much that I hadn't played.

I always tried, during warm-ups, to get my uniform a little dirty. Sometimes Tom let me pitch batting practice, and afterward, on the bench, I would keep my jacket on to look like a pitcher on his day off. I'd sift the dry summer's dust, silken as talc, through my fingers, or make a little pile of it and leave my handprint there.

One afternoon, soon after we arrived at the park from his house, while I was changing my shoes, Tom tossed me a new ball right out of the box. "Loosen up," he said, and turned away. Sick in my stomach, in shock, in some kind of trance, I stared at the ball. I knew he meant that I was to pitch, but I asked him anyway, "What do you mean?"

"You want a written invitation?"

I hardly remember any of it. My father stood behind the screen, behind the batter, the catcher, and the umpire. I was terribly tired, and the ball felt like a heavy stone. I don't remember how many innings I pitched. At one point, as I sat on the bench between innings, I wanted to walk to left field and fall asleep under a big tree out there by Jordan Creek. I wanted to go home and draw pictures in my room. I could hear shrieks and the lifeguard's whistles from the nearby swimming pool, and I wanted to run there and jump from the diving board, knees hugged up against my chest, holding my nose, and sink through the quiet, eyes closed, to the bottom.

One play of that game I will never forget. I walked to the plate without looking behind me at my father, dug in, and hit the first pitch over the second baseman's head. I stood on first base, my blood pounding in my ears. I still didn't look at my father; he was there, a figure behind the backstop, but I didn't look at him. I was going to make him very proud, first; then I would look at him. The pitcher went into his stretch, and I watched his hips, as my father had taught me: "You can always tell if he's going to try to pick you off or throw to the plate. Just watch his hips, not his shoulders, his hips." When the pitcher moved toward the plate, I took off for second base, eyes trained on the bag, and timed my slide perfectly, raising a cloud of silky dust that blew like smoke from an explosion into center field. The second baseman didn't have the ball. "Safe!" I yelled.

"Go back! Go back!" I heard from somewhere. Laughter. Anger. "Go back!" Our catcher, Pete Bachman, was caught between second and third; their third baseman was coming toward him with the ball. For another moment I didn't know what was going on, and then I realized that I had tried to steal second with Pete already there, and had trapped him in this predicament. The third baseman tagged him out, and Pete glared at me, kicked at the dirt, and walked to the bench.

There were two more outs that inning but I don't remember either of them. I stood paralyzed on second base, my face and ears hot. The second baseman and shortstop kept making the safe sign at me while wiggling their knees Charleston-style. The hoots and jeers from the opposing bench were so bad the umpire walked over to put a stop to them. My father was not behind the backstop. I looked until I found him standing behind our bench with his arms crossed, staring at the ground. My stomach felt sick again. My ass hurt now; my anus burned. The one shame left I could prevent was crying, and it took all my power and all my will to do it.

As I walked from the field toward the bench at the end of the inning, I passed Joe Murray, our regular pitcher, heading for the mound. No one spoke to me, and I was too numb to care.

While the game went on loudly, I sat on the bench and arranged the powdery dust with my feet. I bent down and left the print of my hand there, the dust so fine I could see every line of my palm and the whorl of each fingerprint. I knew my father was standing behind me, but I couldn't turn around. I believed that if he knew, he would beat me, and I believed I deserved to be beaten. But Tom had also told me I'd be thrown out of the house, out of my family. He said he knew a kid that this had happened to, and no one had ever heard of him again. "Don't think you're gonna come and live with me, neither," he'd said, as if I would ever have thought of it. It followed that if my father remained my father only because he didn't know the truth, then he wasn't truly my father anymore.

I sat there, hidden in a depth of silence I'd never known until then. I knew I wasn't really safe there, but I was willing to do what was needed, to think or not think any thought, in order to feel, at least for the time being, beyond further hurt, while staring at the image of my hand in the dust.

chapter eight

1960

I HAD SEEN "Men's magazines" before. The barbershop was full of them. When I was younger, seven or eight, I used to page through *Boys' Life* or *Field and Stream* and steal glances at the magazines of the men sitting on either side of me. I wanted to be grown up. Anything that was forbidden me because I was too young, whether by adults or by older kids, offended my sense of fairness. The barbershop was a kind of clubhouse where the men could smoke cigars and pipes and chew Redman tobacco and spit in the filthy dented brass spittoons they slid around the floor with their feet. Vitalis, Brylcreem, Alberto VO5. It never seemed to me that any of the men could possibly need a haircut, so close-cropped were their heads, but they always took their turns, often for a shave, the barber brushing a round cake of soap to a lather in an oversized cup and scraping the straight-edge razor with the pearl handle on the leather strap that hung down from the chair.

"Christ Jesus, will you hurry up."

"Agh, go pound sand up your ass."

"What have you got, some pussy waiting?"

"That's what he's got all right. She's been waiting since Pearl Harbor."

"Hell, you ain't got laid since the last time your sister got drunk."

The barber caught me with *Stag,* or *Mayfair* or something, hidden inside my *Boys' Life*. He must have seen me in the mirror. He snatched the magazine from behind its camouflage and held it up so that the centerfold fell open and hung down, and the men snickered. I sat in the red vinyl chair and tried to pull myself together. There were still two men ahead of me. I couldn't leave; I'd been sent there to get a haircut. The men were laughing and joking; one of them said something about my "little pecker standing up" although it wasn't and it hadn't been. When it was my turn in the barber's chair, he started to put the booster seat in place across the arms, but I made a face and said I didn't need it anymore. I sat up high, holding my rear off the seat by gripping the arms of the chair, and when he draped the striped cloth over me and was fastening it around my neck, I sneaked my foot up under me and sat on my heel.

"I guess you're right," the barber said. "I didn't know you were so tall." He wore a short-sleeved white tunic like a doctor or dentist and, when he reached up to cut my hair, I could see the pale skin of his inner arms, noting that he didn't seem to have much in the way of muscles, and the sweaty dark brush of his armpit. He asked me if my daddy knew how much I liked the girls, and i said, quietly, "I'm sorry. Please don't tell my dad on me."

But he did. Or someone did. My father was enraged.

"You're a little sneak. I can't even send you to the goddamned barbershop. From now on you get your hair cut with your mother."

Dad's stack of magazines was in the bathroom closet, and when I leaned into the dark, blood thumping in my hot red ears, I smelled his after-shave and his sweat. His black gym bag, containing his striped referee's shirt, his black court shoes, and a lanyard I had made for him one rainy day at Jordan Park, was in front of the stack, as if to hide it. I was quiet and alert as a safecracker. I had to remember, even as my hands were shaking with anticipation, even as I warded off the shame I always felt, to return each magazine to its exact place in the stack. It was best to proceed as if my father knew the exact position of each. I believed I was risking everything—my parents' love and my immortal soul—but I was helpless to resist. It seemed to me that everything I wanted or needed was there in that dark corner of the closet. For the next two years or more I pursued my first orgasm to the point of bloodying myself repeatedly in frustration. My body wasn't ready yet. By then I had secrets, I had dreams, I had a room of my own, since Bob could no longer climb the stairs, but my body was no longer mine. No matter how hard or violently I tried, I could not reclaim my body for my own. It was Tom's.

I PULLED ASIDE the heavy purple drape and knelt in the dark closet of the confessional. I could hear talking, murmuring, and I tried hard to keep my mind on my confession and not listen. It was a woman's voice, and I wanted to hear, because I was certain she would be telling the priest about things she'd done with men. I imagined her like the women in Tom's slides and on the playing cards he often carried with him. She probably wore open pink robes with white fur collars and backless high heels. She might be one of those women who could take on three men at once, one in front, one behind, and one with her mouth. I couldn't make out what she was saying. I was sweating, begging my guardian angel to help me pray. Ashamed and inflamed, I bit myself on my arm, hard, to try to drive the pictures from my head. I didn't really want them to go away.

I often gnawed at myself back then. I didn't usually break the skin. Mostly I aggravated the swollen purple crescent with my agonized biting, because it was already tender at that spot and taking the flesh of my arm in my teeth there hurt enough to drive the pictures from my head. I had seen so many naked adults that there were times in school that I even saw the nuns without clothes. I can remember seeing Father Walters mounting Sister Maria Salvatore. I went to the bathroom, sat on the toilet with my feet pulled up so no one would notice me, and bit on my arm until the pounding in my groin was replaced by the pounding in my arm. Sister Maria Salvatore was the tallest woman I knew and she reminded me of the only other very tall woman I had ever seen, in a film Tom had projected on his wall while we were "having fun." The other boys in the sixth grade wondered if Superman could use his X-ray vision to see through women's clothes; I envied him his power to turn it on and off.

One day my mother noticed and asked me about the sore place on my arm. I believe I would have told her everything if I'd had any way to draw the connections among the several worlds I seemed to live in. I was ten years old, maybe eleven, and I couldn't tell my mother that I was gnawing my arm to try to stay in the present, to stay in my child's body, instead of having the small flame of myself engulfed by a fire I took to be damnation. I had been told that the fires of purgatory were different from the fires of hell, and that because the souls in purgatory had not turned their backs on God their suffering was purifying. I had seen pictures of the two places: the devil presided over the fires of hell with a leer on his face, while Jesus himself looked down with compassion on those crying out from purgatory's flames. I was trying to resist. I wasn't turning my back on God. I didn't want to suffer for nothing when I could suffer my way into heaven.

On the other hand, knowing of Tom's pleasure and the release he felt when he "squirted" made me want to squirt too.

Moyer's corner "candy and notions" store had closed and been replaced by a secondhand magazine and comic-book store. Where the candy cases had stood, tempting but padlocked, where Mrs. Moyer's broom swept dust from the raised grain of the dry gray wooden floor that creaked in reliable places, allowing us sometimes to steal rolls of caps for our six-shooters, now there were stacks and stacks of magazines and comic books with the top half of their covers torn off. The store was run by a grimy, pale little man in a Phillies baseball cap. The only other thing you could buy there was bottled Coke that he would fetch from a yellow wooden crate. He would let you sit on the steps and look at comic books without buying any, but for only as long as you could nurse your Coke. When the bottle was empty, he would swoop down on you, reminding you that you hadn't paid the deposit, and grab the bottle and any comic books from your hands. Later on, I remember, a round-shouldered, red Coca-Cola machine appeared on the steps along with scrawled warnings on oak-tag cards taped to the windows and randomly throughout the dusty old store: THIS IS NOT A LIBRARY. BUY HERE—READ HOME. U READ IT—U BOUGHT IT.

I wasn't there to read the comics but to riffle through the stacks until I found an ad I'd seen for 8mm cartoons along with a battery-operated hand-held viewer. "New Technological Breakthrough!" the ad read. "Weighs Less Than a Book! Your Own Private Theater!" I had already begun working to convince my mother how much I liked cartoons. Sometimes she would sing out: "Ah ah ah AH ah, ah ah ah AH ah, that's the Woody Woodpecker song! Ah ah ah AH ah, ah ah ah AH ah, that's the Woody Woodpecker song!" She did a passable Donald Duck voice, and a stuttering Porky Pig: "Aba-dib-aba-dib-aba-dat's all folks!" If I could convince my parents that my love for cartoons was wholesome and boyish, maybe they would let me send away for the viewer. I felt certain I could find a way to borrow movies from Tom's collection. He changed them frequently; so if I could palm one of the small gray plastic spools after he'd projected it, and while we were "having fun," I could take it home and watch it with my hand-held viewer, by myself, in my room, over and over, until I had it more or less memorized. Then I would return it and borrow another and memorize it—until I no longer needed Tom, no longer needed his movies, no longer needed the New Technological Breakthrough! that would Bring the Fun-filled Action Home. Until I could do it all by myself.

My parents weren't hard to fool: I gave them a sunny baseball-playing newsboy, healthy and strong in contrast to Bob and Mike, and hid myself behind report cards. The more ashamed I felt, the better I resolved to be. I lay in my bed at night and bargained with God; my negotiations involved deferred pleasures, promises, sacrifices, pain withstood. I bit my arm and prayed. I promised one day I would be a priest. I begged to be spared. I learned to trade the present for the future.

By the end of the football season, I couldn't bear the shame anymore. I tried to explain to Tom that as a Catholic I would have to tell the priest in confession. I tried to reassure him that he didn't have to worry, that the priest was bound by "the seal of the confessional." Priests had been tortured to death without revealing what was told to them in confession.

"Bullshit," he said. "He'd go right to your mother and father. Think about *that,* you fuckin' little moron. I bet that would go over big, huh?"

After that he avoided me, and only spoke to me when he had to. It was over. I remember a boy named Chris was always with him after that.

So when my mother asked about the purple wound on my arm, I told her a dog had bitten me on my afternoon paper route. She wanted to know whose dog it was. Did it have a collar on? There was no telling what kind of germs a stray might be carrying. As I remember this now, I'm not convinced that she believed me, and thinking of the awful silence that came between us, I sometimes feel as desolate as I did back then, when the winter sky slipped away to dark blue and I hurried to get *The Evening Chronicle* on a mile and a half of doorsteps before it grew too dark to see.

chapter nine

1962

MIKE MADE IT to his feet a few times, but he could only take a couple of steps before he fell. He screamed then, as if he'd broken something, and continued screaming, sometimes banging his head on the floor, until my mother came to gather him up and quiet him. I remember him in his highchair at meals; if he dropped his spoon, he shrieked and rocked and banged his head so hard against the back of the chair that he had lumps. Dad tried to discipline him out of this by removing him from the table, or by threatening to spank him or to take away his crayons and coloring book. Sometimes a little beer in a plastic cup would quiet him. Dad fixed a pad of foam rubber to the back of the highchair with electrician's tape.

Mike stayed in the highchair for a long time. When Bob began to outgrow his wheelchair, Dad bought a larger one, secondhand, from the hospital, and Mike inherited the old one. He never outgrew it.

Mike became a good talker. When it came to TV shows he'd seen, sports events, things that happened at the crippled children's school he attended, or what funny thing

Mom, Dad, Joe, or Bob had said while I was out, he could really make the story come alive again, reaching far back to the details leading to the event, and sometimes losing his audience before he got to the point. He loved company, though we had few visitors during that time.

One day the newsboy was allowed into the living room while Mom went to find some money for him. I was reading and looked up and nodded hello; Bob did the same. The newsboy was uncomfortable with the two wheelchairs. Mom took a long time, and the boy, rocking back and forth and looking at the floor, asked me what I was reading.

"First time he went fishing," Mike said, "he went with Eddie Freeman and his father. You maybe know them if they get the paper from you—oh, that's right, you must. I know they do because Mrs. Freeman asked Mom if she saw in the paper where there was this guy who was grabbing all the ladies uptown in the stores and kissing them. That's right. And they went fishing out near Quakertown, and Eddie caught three big fish and Mr. Freeman put them in a big tub so we could see them still alive when they got home. Bob put his fingers in the water and touched them. Not me; I was too afraid. And Mrs. Freeman said they were dirty fish and they should throw them out, not eat them." Mom came back with the money. As the boy was leaving, Mike shouted after him, "It was Eddie caught all the fish, and that's why Dick keeps reading fishing books!"

His screaming went on and on, mostly at night. The defeats and frustrations of the day became the fears and nightmares that woke us all at night. At first the doctor said that he would outgrow his terror; later he said that it was an electrochemical problem and recommended a diet. Nothing worked.

Sleeping downstairs with him, Bob knew more about Mike's nightmares than the rest of us. Somehow he became used to being awakened by screams a few feet away, and was able to anticipate them. If we slept undisturbed some nights, it was because Bob woke him just before he would have screamed. They talked; there was something between them, sharing the same small room, the same fate, that I can never know. Once I asked Bob if he knew what Mike's nightmares were about. "He's scared," he said.

"But what's he scared of?"

"Nothing. He's just scared. Sometimes it's a clown. He says a big clown laughs and laughs at him and tries to kill him. Once he told me that a puppet chased him and knocked him down and nailed him to the floor. Another time he told me there were worms in his bed. He's just scared, that's all." He gave me a look then, as if he were going to go on, but he didn't.

chapter ten

1962

WHEN I WAS thirteen, my grandfather died, and we moved into his house on Thirteenth Street, an old row house with stained glass, dormers, a front porch, a fireplace, and, to this day, certain smells that remind me of my grandparents. My father spent several months of evenings and weekends renovating. I was excited when my father and his friends knocked down the wall between the kitchen and the dining room; it was bold, a gesture, also disturbing and sacrilegious. I remember how much my dad, with his hair full of plaster dust, resembled my grandfather.

The wall was removed to make a downstairs room for Mike and Bob. It was a simple project: Dad sectioned off half the dining room with a frame of two-by-fours covered with inexpensive paneling and fitted with louvered folding doors. The other half was just large enough for two cots and the commode. We also built a ramp to fit tightly over the back steps for my brothers' wheelchairs. Dad built this mostly by himself; my job was to sort through a coffee can of nails and straighten out the bent ones on the sidewalk.

"Nails don't grow on trees," my father said. When the ramp was finished, with raised wooden slats for footing in the center, we painted it gray. We made other changes at the house before we moved in: paint, wallpaper, panelling, a dropped ceiling, carpeting on the stairs, but we were especially proud of the small room and the ramp.

My brother Mike continued to scream. Sometimes he screamed at what he saw on television; if anyone started shouting he'd begin to shriek and rock and bang his head.

Probably what Mike feared most was the lift: an ugly cast-iron derrick which transferred him from bed to wheelchair to commode. Heavy chains hung from the crossbar and hooked onto pieces of canvas that made a precarious seat. When you pumped a lever, the jangling chains tightened and lifted and swung him over the commode. He cried and trembled. My father sympathized with him and swore at the "god-damned fuckin' thing"; he hated it for other reasons. It took too long to place the canvas properly, hook up the chains, maneuver the whole thing and slowly release the pressure; then the canvas had to be unhooked and pulled out from under. It was much easier and faster simply to grab Mike or Bob under the arms and heave.

I remember my father coming in the front door, pulling off his coat. "Come on. Let's go! Come on."

"I don't think I have to go," Bob would say.

"Well damn it, you're gonna sit there then," my father would say, slapping off the wheelchair's brakes, and pushing him into the small room. Mom would tell him, "Careful of your back," and he would snap at her, "What do you *want* me to do—you want to lift him?—then shut up for god's sake." I'd get angry. Bob would say, "I'm sorry. I can't help it." Mike would cry. Joe most times would go out on the porch or upstairs to his room. Dad would come back later in the evening, long enough to take Bob off and put Mike on the commode. On some of his jobs he had to have someone lie for him to get the twenty minutes.

In high school I involved myself in every activity I could, mostly sports but also the orchestra, the school newspaper, and the chorus. Joe was still very young but old enough to carry the pot upstairs, dump it in the toilet, and rinse it under the bathtub faucet. One day I was walking down the street and saw Joe come out of the house, slam the door, and stomp down the front steps, wiping his eyes with his wrists. When I walked in the house, my father was lifting Mike back into his wheelchair from the commode. "Your brother thinks he's too damn good to have to help around here," he said. One thing you never said around my father: *Why do I always have to be the one to do it?*

chapter eleven

1964

MY MOTHER WAS always puzzled when people expressed their admiration: "How did you do it?" She didn't know. It was the wrong question, and when asked in the past tense, it was doubly wrong and painful. "You just do it," she would say.

She never imagined another life. The future was foreordained. She held to a pathetic sliver of hope for a medical discovery, but dreams of a different life were useless self-indulgence.

She had been a singer. I don't believe she ever meant to make a career of it, but she had sung in local bars and clubs during the war. When I was little, she sang show tunes all day: "When You Walk Through a Storm," "Moon River," "Apple Blossom Time." She liked Sinatra, Perry Como, Johnny Horton. She stopped singing; I don't remember exactly when. The record player broke and was never repaired. Except for the offerings on TV, our house was without music.

Weekdays began at five. She perked the coffee, then woke my father. She woke Bob and Mike and dressed them in their beds (without pulling up their pants, because when Dad came downstairs it was time for them to use the commode). She packed five lunches, woke Joe and me, and served breakfast. By seven Dad had placed my brothers in their wheelchairs and gone to work. Joe or I would empty the pot upstairs, the other helping Mom to get Bob or Mike into their coats and hats. At seven-thirty the school bus came. It was a yellow van with flashing lights, CAUTION: CRIPPLED CHILDREN painted on the front and back, and with a wheelchair lift built onto the right side. Joe and I then left for school. Except for those days when she went shopping, Mom stayed home; she didn't watch much television and she wasn't much of a reader. She cleaned, sewed, baked, and did laundry till we returned from school.

Now I understand my father better: sometimes he wanted out.

One evening, when I was fifteen, I came home to my mother sitting alone in the living room. Bob and Mike were already in bed; Joe was staying with a cousin. I could see that she'd been crying. While I was hanging my jacket in the closet, she said, "Your father's gone."

"Where?"

"Gone!" she said.

"What are you talking about?"

"He found some woman and he says he loves her."

"That's ridiculous! What happened?"

"He wants to send your brothers to the Good Shepherd Home. I won't! I won't!" she cried and grabbed my arm. "Help me. Don't let him send them away."

I hated him then, but I wanted to go away myself and have another life as much as he did.

He came in that night, very late, and slept on the sofa.

In the morning he lifted my brothers into their wheelchairs. No one said a word until Bob cried out, "Don't send us to a home! Don't go away, Dad. Please!"

"I'll be good, Dad. I'll be good," Mike cried.

My father slammed his fist into the wall and kicked over a chair. "*God damn* it!" he shouted. "I'm not some fuckin' superman! What kind of life is this? I'm thirty-six years old! What kind of life is this? You'll be the death of me, all of you!" He jumped up and down and screamed and knocked things over. Mom and Joe stood in the corner. Everyone was crying but me; I didn't know what to do but stay out of his way. By then I had come to understand something about my father: there were two of him. It seemed there had always been two of him: even when we were little, when he was the man who let Bob and me ride "horsey" on his back, he was also the man who, on other days, raged and hit and kicked us when he came home from working at the brewery. He was the man I loved and the man I feared; a pair of images in the Viewmaster that I fumbled with, never quite able to click them into one.

He became more and more enraged, cursing and swearing, knocking flowerpots and figurines from the windowsill. "I can't take it anymore!" he shouted. He backed against the wall and slid down it till he was sitting on the floor among uprooted houseplants, shards, and dirt, with his knees drawn up and his face in his hands, crying quietly and repeating, "I can't. I can't. I can't."

After a few moments, Mom nudged Joe toward me; I put my hand on his shoulder as she went to Dad. I was afraid he might blow up at her. She knelt next to him and took his head in her arms, and they cried. My father said, "I'm sorry. I'm sorry."

He called in sick that day, and when the yellow school bus pulled up in front of the house, he waved it on. He played cards and checkers with Bob and Mike all day and told them again and again that he would never send them away. Never.

chapter twelve

1970

THE LAST I saw of my brother Mike alive, he was being kept alive by a number of machines: oxygen through a small green piece of plastic tubing under his nostrils, an I.V. in his arm, a catheter in his penis to collect his urine in a small bag that hung next to the bed, electrodes taped to his chest so that we could see his heartbeat blipping on a small screen. He never came out from under the anesthesia after his operation. The burst appendix was only a sign. The doctor told us that his pH balance was so acidic that there was little or no chance of correcting it, although they were trying. So of course we all believed in that one chance; I remember fixing on the image of a small boat at sea, almost capsized, tipping over, but maybe . . .

In the middle of the night the phone rang. I answered it. The nurse said we could come in the morning.

I went upstairs, where my parents were sitting on the edge of their bed, sobbing. I stood in the doorway, numb, and looked at them. Then I thought of Bob. He must have heard the phone and understood.

He was in his room downstairs, in his bed. I went in,

turned on the lamp, sat down on the bed, and took his hand. He was not crying; he was shaking. I started to tell him that it was just that Mike's appendix had burst before they had a chance to remove it, and that, and that . . . and he looked at me and said, "Cut the shit, Dick," and kept shaking. Then we both cried hard. I started sobbing, and he cried quietly, lying on his back, the tears running down into his ears.

When we went to the hospital the next morning, there were no more tubes, no more electrodes, catheters, hookups; just Mike lying there, looking calm, in a horrible parody of sleep.

I WENT WITH my father to pick out a casket. It was like buying a car. A showroom of empty caskets with silk pillows, silk linings: mahogany caskets with brass pipes around them; rose-colored caskets of steel with handles, three to a side and one on each end; dull nickel-colored ones with powder-blue silk linings, and so forth. I despised the small man who showed us around and walked with little shuffling steps, bent over, holding his hands together as he spoke very quietly, making little bows as we stopped in front of each casket and rubbing his hands together like a fly. You had to ask how much they were, because he did not talk money, saying only, "Now for a little more we have this to offer, very nice, very tasteful . . . and of course if you prefer less of an expense we offer this one, also very nice, very nice." And when we asked him how much, he would turn over a little card on the pillow, and the price would be written there. He would make his half-bow again, hands together, and wait. When we walked on, he would turn the card facedown again. My father's stoicism was, I knew, an effort, and he made a selection by saying, "This will do," touching one of them quickly and turning away.

"And a crucifix?" the man said. "You'll find them in this case over here," and he began to lead us, but I saw my father begin shaking his head, the tears welling up in his eyes again, and I said to the man, "We're going now," steering my father to the door. "Pick something nice; it doesn't matter."

"Yes, yes, I'm sorry, I understand, I understand."

WHEN BOB DIED we called the man and told him we wanted exactly the same thing.

chapter thirteen

1972

THE FACT THAT I had come all the way from Boston where I'd moved right after college, and on such short notice, confirmed what Bob had already grasped. I don't remember how I greeted him. There was terror in his eyes. I felt as if I were bringing him the news of his death.

He was propped in the bed, his hands limp at his sides; under the covers, the soles of his feet were together and his knees splayed. For a moment I saw him as a stranger might, and I realized how years in his wheelchair had left him misshapen and how horribly his disease had weakened him. The muscles of his back could not support him, and he was kept in the middle of the bed by pillows on both sides. His legs were thin, atrophied, and his heavy sagging trunk tapered upward to his frail, bony shoulders and useless arms. He had trouble holding up his head. He hadn't been shaved in a couple of days, and I noticed that his beard grew mostly under his chin, like mine.

Mom and Dad stood by the bed. Dad said, "You see, your brother Dick's here now. Everything's going to be all right." Then he looked at me as if to ask forgiveness for saying such a stupid thing.

"You going to stay awhile?" Bob asked me.

"Few days," I said. "Until you're better." The look he gave me made me turn my head away. I had betrayed him. I promised myself I wouldn't lie to him again.

My father went to the door and motioned for me to join him. There was a sofa at the end of the hall, with Dad's overcoat balled at one end to serve as a pillow; he had tried to get Mom to sleep a bit last night.

"I'm glad you're here. We didn't think he'd make it through last night. Have you eaten? There's a coffee shop downstairs. Maybe you should go down and get us some sandwiches. They're probably open by now. If you just want coffee, there's a machine at the other end of the hall." He took out his wallet, and his hands were shaking.

"Dad," I said and touched him on the arm. He stopped a moment; then he let out a sob and hugged me, crying hard. My father is a big, heavy man and so much taller than me that when I try to comfort him, it's always my head on his shoulder. We sat on the sofa. "This is it," he said. "This is really it." We had expected this so long, and yet we were astonished.

The light above the door to Bob's room was flashing, and a nurse came running down the hall. We ran back to the room. The nurse was readying a suction catheter to enable Bob to breathe more freely. He gagged as she eased the plastic tube up through his nose and down his throat. Dad and I held him upright. He looked from one to the other of us, scared. Mom turned away and covered her face. The nurse withdrew the tube and wheeled the portable unit into the corner. "Thanks," Bob said to her, "that's better." He needed the machine often after that, and he came to welcome its relief. During his last hours, early the next day, he asked for it when it was useless; he was confident that it could help him.

He could not find comfort; ten minutes in any position was all that he could bear. He said his skin hurt. "Move me! Move me!" he cried out. He insisted that my father move him; he said the nurses didn't do it right and that I was too rough. His discomfort went on until my father couldn't lift him anymore. Dad was beaten and crying. "Bob, please," he said, "no matter where I put you it still hurts. Please try to bear it. Let Dick try it. Your mother. The two of them together. Try it. I can't lift you anymore. I can't."

He was given drugs for the pain, but they made him sleepy and he was afraid to sleep. "I won't wake up," he said. His resistance to sedatives was magnificent. He asked for coffee. I left the room and went to the coffee machine. I planned to be gone long enough for the sedative to take effect. I stood at the machine and waited, worrying that I was betraying him again. I thought of his pain, his inability to relax, his fear of sleep, and I waited. I drank a cup myself before I finally put another quarter in the machine and carried the cup back to the room.

Bob was delirious. He was talking but the voice wasn't his. The talk came from childhood: "One potato, two potato, three potato, four . . ." and a little tune: "Shave 'n' a haircut, five cents!" My mother held his hand, crying, and a tiny laugh came through her sobs at the memory of the tune. It was part of a song Dad used to sing to us when we were little. Dad took the coffee I had brought. He told me that he thought that this was the end. He said that it was good, that Bob was happy.

Bob squeezed his eyes shut tight, fighting the drug. He relaxed, but as soon as he had dozed off, he woke and looked around the room. When he saw me, he asked if I had brought his coffee. I looked at Dad, who said, "You were asleep, and it was getting cold, so I drank it."

"I'll get you another cup," I said, and started for the door, but Bob said, "Never mind. It's lousy coffee anyway."

Well into the night, he was given pain medication, which he always managed to keep from putting him to sleep. He was weakened to the point of dying, but until his final surrender, he did not sleep during the thirty-six hours we were with him.

Nurses came and went; we didn't pay much attention to them. Once I got it through my head that Bob knew he was dying, I was awed. I believe he saw that we were sometimes more afraid than he was. "The doctor told me the Phillies lost again. They got the pitching. Got nobody who can hit the ball." He said that for Dad, who disagreed: "They hit okay, but never when it counts. You know they left eleven runners on base Monday night? That's some kind of record."

"And the errors hurt them," Mom said.

"What's the use of hitting if you can't hit in the clutch?" said Bob.

By nightfall we were all exhausted. No one wanted to leave the room, but the night nurse insisted that, until morning, only one of us could be in the room at a time. My father was about to lose his temper, and my mother was shocked at the woman's insensitivity. I was angry too, and I followed the nurse down the hall to her station.

"I don't believe you people!" I railed at her. "My brother is dying. We want to be with him. What kind of rule forbids a family's being with the dying? You think you're God or something? You take your god-damned rule and shove it! Who the hell do you think you are?"

She was sitting at a low counter, writing in a chart, and she looked up, pointed her pen at me, and said in a loud whisper, "You think there's a rule? There is no rule. Now listen. You know your brother won't get well. I'm sorry. I really am. But stop and think about your parents. Do you know what they're going to go through after this? You may be young and strong enough to stay up every night till this is over, but your mother . . ."

"Hold it," I said. "Okay." I remembered Mike's funeral, and knew very well what the next week would be like. I went back to the room and told my parents I couldn't get the nurse to budge.

Mom managed to sleep, and we didn't disturb her. Dad took over for me sometime in the middle of the night, and I began my second watch at about five o'clock.

The dark of the lounge, Mom's quiet snoring, the plan of a rotating watch, was some comfort. When I entered the room, I wasn't ready. Bob was staring straight ahead at something I couldn't see. His mouth was twisted in a snarl, his eyes were fierce, and his face was red with anger. He seemed so far away that I said, "Bob. Bob. It's me. Dick."

"Water," he said. I filled a paper cup and held it to his lips. When he finished drinking, he said, "What was the name that Dad made up for the ghost? Remember? When we were scared? He told us not to worry when we heard a scary noise. A woman's name."

"He always told us it was 'Maggie-behind-the-wallpaper.'"

"That's right." He sighed. "I thought it was something more profound than that." He began to laugh.

"I don't get it," he said.

"Get what?" I asked.

"Why can't I find the words?" he said. He laughed again and then was quiet. For three or four hours I watched a pulse in his neck. It was like holding his heart in my hands. When it stopped, I went out into the hall and hugged my mother. At first she hugged me back; then she held me at arm's length and looked in my eyes. I didn't nod or anything but she broke into tears and slumped against me, and I lowered her till she was sitting on the floor in the hospital corridor, rocking and crying. My father leaped up—"No No No No No"—and ran into the room.

"Don't be afraid. Don't be afraid," I had whispered in his ear, keeping my vigil at the pulse in his neck. I don't know if he heard me.

I drove the car home, eyes on the traffic, Mom and Dad, their faces red, held each other in the back seat, moaning and crying out from time to time, "Bob!"

chapter fourteen

1975

THERE IS LITTLE that speaks of the lives of my brothers in our house. The makeshift downstairs bedroom became a sewing room; the ramp is long gone from the back porch. On one wall of the living room we hung the two small crucifixes from my brothers' caskets, but soon there was new furniture in the room, and it was arranged differently, no longer leaving room for two wheelchairs. It was as if the house belonged to some other family.

Some years ago, on a visit home, during a fitful night sleeping on the convertible sofa in the living room, I woke tangled in the sheets and lying across the bed so that the first thing I saw was the pair of bronze-on-silver crucifixes on the wall above me. I didn't think of either of my brothers; I thought of how their wheelchairs, the brown one and the green one, had been transformed into these two crosses, as if that had been their fate all along.

Later that day I went down to the cellar, for the first time in years, to look for an old fishing reel of mine. It was a hot afternoon, and the cool of the cellar was pleasant; the small street-level windows, cobwebbed and cloudy with dirt, filtered soft gray light over everything. Under one window was the blue Formica table where as a teenager I had spent many hours alone tying trout flies, building model planes, or examining ants, flies, or pond water with my Gilbert microscope. My homemade barbells, pieces of pipe with cans of cement on the ends, were propped in the corner by the tool closet.

Inside the closet, the old bait-casting reel was on a shelf among my father's tools, an old brown baseball, jars of nuts and bolts and cans of nails. The reel was rusty but still turned; it needed oil. The line had rotted on the spool and would have to be cut off. I picked up the baseball and remembered how my father used to take a brush and scrub the horsehide with bleach to get it white again.

My mother had gone shopping; if she had been upstairs, she would have called to me, "What happened? You get lost down there?" For years I came down here for peace and solitude. Tying a Royal Coachman or a Bucktail, I could feel my fly rod flex with the fight of a big brown trout; looking at amoebas in a drop of water, I imagined myself a scientist searching for a cure for muscular dystrophy.

I saw the rear wheel, blue fender and red reflector of my bicycle jutting from behind what used to be the coalbin at the far end of the cellar. I walked past the oil burner and around the bin. My bicycle, with the handlebars wrenched crooked and both tires flat, leaned against the wall; next to it were the wheelchairs, folded, the footrests turned up, brakes locked. Nearby were my brothers' cots, also folded; and the commode, open, without its pot; and the lift, attached from its chains to the wall by cobwebs.

I remembered my father's struggles to raise money for these things and felt anger at their waste. They should have been given away, donated to some agency. I felt an urge to pull out my bicycle, straighten the handlebars, see if the tires would hold air, but I couldn't get to it without moving the wheelchairs. I couldn't bring myself to move them. On the floor were schoolbooks and notebooks, coloring books, and the baseball-score books that Bob had kept of years of televised games. I remembered his knowledge of baseball; he could give you the statistics on nearly every player in the major leagues. A daddy long-legs walked along the armrest of the smaller of the two wheelchairs.

I couldn't disturb a thing.

MY MOTHER KEPT a battered shoe box full of photographs; the corners had been taped again and again. The lid was kept on with rubber bands. If you emptied the photographs from the box it collapsed completely. One year I bought an album for her for her birthday: "Now you can throw away that busted-up old shoe box," I said when she unwrapped it. She never used it. Even a new shoe box would have seemed wrong to her.

. . . Mammy Etta, young, squinting into the sun, her face too dark to see. My mother as a little girl, her face scratched out and scribbled over with a red crayon. My twin aunts, Marie and Marietta, in high school, bobby sox and saddle shoes. A tiny box-camera snapshot, hardly more than an inch square, of Mom and Dad hugging on a park bench during their engagement. My mother with the four of us, her eyes rolled up comically, in make-believe exasperation. Several pictures of Bob and me together, playing. My First Communion, in my white suit. Bob's First Communion in the same white suit. Me in my baseball uniform. Bob sitting in a red wagon . . .

There's a picture of Bob and me sitting on the bed in our room in the house on Ninth Street; we must be about six and seven years old. He reached up and put rabbit ears on me. I punched him on the arm for that, and he cried. It was probably a rainy day—we rarely spent time in our room otherwise, except when we were sleeping or being punished.

Dad never tolerated lying. When he asked us who broke the window, who stomped all over the neighbors' flowers, who tore all the pictures out of his baseball magazine before he had a chance to read it, and if neither of us confessed, he sent us to our room, without toys, until one of us came out with the truth. We were afraid of him. Sometimes, after a while, he would come into our room and sit down on the bed and talk with us, explaining that when you do something wrong you should be man enough to admit it. Other times he would shout a warning: "You better have an answer before I come up there!" And Bob and I would argue even more feverishly about who was to blame, afraid this would be one of those times when Dad would pull his belt through his belt loops like a man drawing a sword and order us to drop our pants. Then it was too late.

I remember at least once when we struck a deal. I was invited to go to a Phillies game with my friend Pete and his father, and I knew that if I admitted to whatever I had done (I don't remember what), I wouldn't be allowed to go. Bob said he'd done it. We agreed that I owed him the next one. I went to the game. I think my father knew, because Bob wasn't punished after all.

Bob and I in the backyard; we're about six and seven —these are some of the last pictures of us together. We've each just had one of Dad's haircuts, the line, across our foreheads straight, angling right to left. The smiles on our faces are unreal, a reply to "Say cheese," but the yard behind us—bats, balls, and gloves, cap guns, a spilled peach basket of toys—is alive with memories.

The yard was ours together: there was onion grass to chew on, crickets to trap under our hands, buttercups, morning glories climbing the fence near the shed, salamanders under rocks, tiger lilies in the far corner near the rusty post, dandelions my mother boiled and ate for lunch. There was something damp and erotic about the rose of Sharon that grew by the shed; when the blossoms closed and fell on the ground they looked, to Bob and me, like so many veined purple-blue "peepees." After a day or two, they turned brown and mushy and neither of us wanted to touch them. We wanted to know why there were always black ants on the peonies, and how lightning bugs worked. We caught them and kept them in jars. Bob smeared one on the wall of the shed; it left a phosphorescent streak. He wanted to catch enough of them to print his name on the wall, but Mom said that wasn't nice, that we could catch them but we shouldn't hurt them. Both of us thought that was stupid, since they always died in the jar anyway, despite the holes we punched in the lid. We smeared our names, small, on the short concrete walk in the yard, but they only shone for a few minutes.

And the neighbors' yards: the wire fences served as nothing but reminders that we were off-limits. Usually it was permissible to cross to retrieve a ball from either of our next-door neighbors' yards, so we often threw one over the fence to legitimize a raid on the Schanks' cherry tree. On the other side, the Zimmermans had red and white roses. We ate some of those too—one petal at a time, with salt from a little disposable lunchbox shaker. We argued which were tastier; I liked the red ones, Bob preferred the white.

The grass grew tall in the yard behind ours. We were afraid of the man who lived there. Once, Dad had a fight with him. They stood at the fence and swore at each other. The man threatened Dad, who picked up one of our baseball bats and laughed at him. Mom came out. "Put down that bat!" she said to my father and started yelling at the man about his messy yard and house and about keeping our balls whenever they went in his yard and that he shouldn't scare Bob and me, we were only children, and that it was no wonder his wife had left him in his ugly house all by himself. The fight had started because the man made Dad pay for a window we'd broken and then only patched it with cardboard.

THERE ARE TWO small snapshots of Bob and me, aged four and five, in our plastic wading pool in the yard. In one of them Bob is holding a plastic boat above his head and glaring at me; I am looking at the camera. We must have been fighting over it when I stopped to smile and pose. Timmy, a playmate from up the block, is also in the picture; he is not in the pool, though. It was the time of the polio scare, and his mother wouldn't allow him in the pool with us. At the time, people believed that water left standing for any length of time bred crippling germs. That's what had happened to all those people with braces and crutches or in wheelchairs; they'd been swimming in stagnant water. Sometimes Bob and I would splash Timmy, who'd back off, yelling, "Stop it! That's polio water! Cut it out!" At least once we sent him home crying. I remember he lost a sneaker climbing the fence in panic; Bob grabbed it and jumped back in the pool with a big splash. I took the sneaker, dunked it, and threw it at Timmy; he wouldn't touch it. He shouted that he was going to tell his father and we'd have to buy him a new pair of sneakers. "And I hope you both get crippled up with polio!" he yelled.

In the other photo, I'm in the pool and Bob is lying on the concrete walk that jutted out past the toolshed into the yard. On cool days we would do that: the concrete held the heat, and it felt good to lie on our bellies and be warmed. When we rose, our shadows, made of water, were left on the walk. By the time they dried and faded, we were cold enough and the walk was warm enough to lie on again. On hot days we had to run from the pool to the shade by the house. I don't know why the walk was there; it reached a third of the way into the yard and stopped. Sometimes we pretended that it was a dock, and the rest of the yard was water filled with alligators and man-eating fish, and we'd try to push each other from it.

Several years ago, on a visit home, I sat in the kitchen looking through the shoe box with my mother. Most of the pictures were facedown, so looking through them was like turning over cards. I came to understand why my mother never used the album I'd bought her. To arrange the pictures chronologically, or any other way, would be a fiction. A memory is something that happens. To arrange memories in a particular order is to protect oneself, to substitute form for feeling. Better to reach in the box and pick a card at random. My mother's shoe box was an emblem of her courage.

I turned over a snapshot taken on my First Communion day. My head and shoulders almost fill the picture, but I'm out of focus. On the concrete walk, very small in the background, just below my right ear, Bob has fallen and is trying to get back on his feet. I remembered those times, how Bob spoke to himself, impatient but encouraging, "Come on now, *push*. Now keep your balance, *nnnh*. Good. There. Okay."

And I remembered other times, when I was responsible for bringing Bob home from school. I was in fourth grade, he in third. By then he walked on his toes; the tendons of his calves were tightening, pulling his heels off the ground. And I remember one day in particular: Bob is on the ground; I want to get home because I'm supposed to play football with Pete and his friends. They've never asked me to play with them before, and Bob is ruining everything. I grab him by the arm; he screams and won't let me pull him to his feet. I hit him. He cries. I try to pull him up and he screams again. I kick him. He lies there and cries among the horse-chestnut cases and yellow leaves stuck to the sidewalk on Ninth Street. A neighbor called my parents. My father said he'd "beat me within an inch of my life" if I ever laid a hand on Bob again.

I was holding the picture and shaking. I handed it to my mother. "Oh, who took this one? You're all blurry," she said. If she noticed the scene in the background, she didn't comment; she turned it facedown on the pile of those she'd already looked at. "Here's a good one of Bob," she said. He is sitting in his chair, a blank look on his face, at the end of the concrete walk, where we always wheeled him when he wanted to be outdoors.

chapter fifteen

1984

I FLEW HOME several times during the months of my mother's last illness, sometimes with my wife and baby, other times alone. Maybe because I didn't fly until I was in my twenties, I tend to think of airports and planes in terms of adventure and excitement, but since that time I've noticed that among the hurrying business travelers and the oddly dressed vacationers there are always two or three whose eyes are red from crying, who have the vacant look one wears containing grief in public. On one occasion I went to buy some Rolaids at a candy counter, and there among the key chains, T-shirts, magazines, and Smurf dolls, I began to cry. An eruption; there was no stanching it. And a man in a trench coat was suddenly at my elbow, handing me a tissue and the small package it came from, which he had just purchased. While I blew my nose, he picked up his bag and sped away. I pulled myself together and bought the Rolaids, which I needed because I wanted to drink, both before and during the flight.

I have a page from a journal written during one of these flights:

I want to grab this guy in front of me and yell, "We're eighteen thousand feet up bucking like a Yugo on a dirt road and most of your hair's already fallen out no matter how you try to grease and comb it and you're reading a Xeroxed manual on *Greater Product Definition in Market Segments Previously Dormant!*"

And the old priest next to me is wearing diocesan-issue glasses: black frames, clear rims, with a little metal chevron at the hinge, and he slumps against me, asleep.

There are four hundred thirty-seven rivets visible from seat 17A on the wing engine manifold of a 737. I want another vodka.

MY MOTHER WAS in the hospital two days before my father could bring himself to say the word "cancer." "But they don't have all the tests yet," he said.

"How's she doing? How's she feeling?"

"Jesus Christ, you know what your mother says to me? I ask her does she want anything from home and she tells me a carton of cigarettes! Fuckin' cigarettes!"

He was angry. He already knew she was leaving him.

FOR A TIME after my mother's death, I hated old women who smoked. I wanted to scream at them: "How dare you smoke and get away with it and grow old enough to tint your hair blue and be a grandmother to someone who will grow up to remember you?"

Robert likes to look through the album of our wedding pictures. He used to ask, "Who that lady?"

"That's your grandma who died. You don't remember her, but she loved you very much."

"Why she die?"
"She was very sick."
"Why?"
Later he would point to her in the picture and call her "my-grandma-who-died."
"That's right."
"I want to see her."
"Well there she is. In the picture."
"But why I can't see her?"

ONE MORNING, WHEN Robert was small enough to hold in the crook of my arm, my lips against his silky head, I dozed and dreamed that he and I were at an outdoor celebration. There was a big yellow-and-white-striped tent like the one Kathi and I had at our wedding. I was holding Robert proudly. People bent to him and touched and patted me, nodding and smiling. We were seated at a very long table, across from a radiant old man. I asked him why we were celebrating, and he said there was no occasion, that he and all the others were always there; didn't I know that? I suddenly felt that I did. I propped Robert in his little plastic seat on the table. "We're always here; we're family," the old man said, touching Robert and smiling at me.

The food was delicious. The baked beans were my mother's. She used to make them for picnics when I was a boy. I wanted more. The food was under the yellow-and-white-striped tent. I heaped the plate high and ate some right away, on my way back to the table.

They were gone, all of them. Robert's yellow seat was on the table, empty. Oh no. Oh no no no no no. Again I felt that I knew what had happened. I saw the old man, in the distance, walking away. "Wait!" I called, and ran to catch up to him.

He turned and said, coldly, what I fully expected to hear. "You didn't take care of him, so he's been taken from you." I tried to grab the old man, but I fell, helpless, and lay on the ground.

I woke, and Robert stirred in the hollow underneath my chin but remained asleep, his tiny mouth making sucking movements. He had given me the dream as a gift: without the small warmth of him to wake to, reassured, I would never have let myself have that dream. I would never have been able to feel, if only briefly, the horror and despair and shame of losing him. For the first time, I touched, for merely a dreaming moment, the kind of pain my parents must have felt, grieving for my brothers.

AT LAST THE call from the hospital came; Mom was in the Recovery Room. The surgeons had removed her right lung. Later we received another call informing us that she was no longer in Recovery, and we could see her briefly. My father grabbed his jacket, fished in his pocket for the car keys, threw them to me.

At the front door to the hospital, Dad fell behind, and I was through the automatic door before I noticed. I turned and saw him standing against a concrete post with his head down. I turned back, but the door was one-way and I had to go through the revolving door. When I touched his arm and asked if he was okay, he lifted his head, jaws clenched, face red and wet, and said, through his teeth, "I've spent half my life in this fuckin' hospital."

Joe was already upstairs. He told us we had to wait until the hour, when we could see her, one at a time, for a total of ten minutes. "Oh, what kind of bullshit is this now," Dad said, grabbing the handle of the heavy door. It was locked.

"You have to ring the bell," Joe said.

"Wait," I said. "It's twenty of."

My father was leaning against the door, cupping his hands around the small window, looking in. Through the window of the other door, I could see nothing but the curtains around each bed, a nurse in a lab coat carrying a small tray, one machine with tiny red lights and gauges and wires plugged into it like a switchboard.

Dad went in first. When he returned to the corridor, I asked him if Mom was awake. He covered his face with his hand and nodded, and I walked past him.

I'd forgotten to ask which bed was Mom's, and I walked down the center aisle looking to both sides. I remember seeing one patient, man or woman I couldn't tell, mouth gaping, eyes wide open. He or she could not have weighed a hundred pounds. I almost passed my mother's bed; the curtains were parted only the width of a doorway. For a moment I wasn't sure it was she. Her mouth was open wide around a blue plastic hose connected to a machine at the head of her bed. *Whoosh. Click.* Her face was white and wet with perspiration, and her hair, fanned out around her on the pillow, was grayer than she'd ever let us see, only the last couple of inches still colored black. Her eyes were closed; when I touched her hand, they opened quickly and rolled in panic until she found me. She gripped my thumb, and I was startled and reassured by the strength in her hand. But I felt her desperation in her grip. "You made it," I said.

A week later she came home from the hospital, minus

one lung, and her voice was barely audible because the surgeons had had to scrape the spreading cancer from her larynx. Tipping up her oxygen mask to speak, she held out her hand to me. "Look at my fingers," she rasped. "They're not yellow anymore. I quit."

I WAS SITTING on a kitchen chair next to her bed in the makeshift room. It was night. My father, brother, wife, and baby son were asleep upstairs. The only sounds in the house were the bubbling plastic cup on the oxygen compressor and the sibilance of my mother's shallow breathing. Her face changed, continually, as I watched. From time to time she mumbled something and I leaned close to her.

"I know," she said, softly. "I know. I lose. But don't do this to me. Who are these people? No, I paid. Tell him I paid. I won't do that. No, not unless you show it to me first. Ah. It's beautiful."

Another time she whispered, fiercely, "No! Let go of me. Don't touch me!" And when I released her hand, her eyes opened wide and she grabbed for me in panic. "No no, not you, not you."

A coughing spasm woke her. Her grip hurt my hand. She pressed the button to raise herself in the bed, plucked at pink tissues in a box beside her, and coughed. She let go of my hand a moment and with a frantic gesture let me know that I should switch the green plastic tube from the compressor to the tall tank in the corner that put out more oxygen. I started to rise, but she grasped my arm and shook her head. "Mom, I can't switch it over without getting up." Her nails dug into my wrist. She was choking. Shaking her head. Crying.

Once she asked for her mirror. "Wait till your brothers get a load of this," she said to me, staring at herself.

"Don't you have a holy candle?" Aunt Kitty asked.

"Agh!" my father said. "A holy candle. How the hell should I know?"

"She should have a holy candle when she crosses." She spoke as an exasperated adult speaks to a difficult child. "It isn't right. She has to have a holy candle burning when she crosses."

"Hold on," I said. I went upstairs to my parents' bedroom, where I knew I would find two blessed candles inside the hollow mahogany crucifix above their bed. When I took it down, the plaster behind it crumbled and the nail it had hung on fell down inside the wall. I touched the cracked and yellowed ivory Jesus and then pressed upward gently until the cross slid away, tongue-in-groove, to reveal a compartment containing a vial each of holy water and holy oil, both dry now, two candles, short, wicks burnt, and a slot into which the crucifix could be placed upright. I hadn't handled it since I was a boy, when someone, maybe my mother, showed it to Bob and me; we'd been curious about it because at school we were learning about the sacraments. The one called Extreme Unction scared us. We wondered if you had to die once the priest anointed you with the holy oil. Was it too late then to get better? What if the priest was too anxious and wanted to hurry up and get someplace else? Bob and I called it the death kit. We invested it with mystery: it could keep away devils and protect you from hell, but once you invoked its power you had to die.

I couldn't decide whether to bring the whole kit downstairs or just one candle. I took one candle from its cavity and began to slide the crucifix back into place; then I did a curious, reflexive thing: I held the candle to my nose and smelled it. It *was* my mother who showed this to us; I remembered her explaining to us, with her convert's zeal and awe, that only candles made of pure beeswax could be blessed by the priest and made holy. "You can always tell a real beeswax candle," she said, and after drawing one under her nose with her eyes closed, "Hmmmmmm," she held it out for Bob and me to smell. I put the candle back, slid Jesus back in place, and brought the whole cross downstairs.

I WAS ABOUT to put on my coat. I needed to get outside, once around the block, fresh air. Aunt Kitty waved me to her, put her hand on my arm. "Stay." I went back into the small room and knelt by the side of the bed. Dad placed my hand on Mom's leg. It was cold. Both Dad and Aunt Kitty nodded when I looked at them. I felt my mother's wrist for a pulse; for a moment I was sure I felt one, then there was none. Within moments the cold crept up her body as if death were pulling a blanket over her.

My father rested his forehead on the bed beside her, and I stroked his back and rested my hand on the back of his neck. I remember that my relief, after such a long struggle, was so great that I had a strange impulse to congratulate my mother for what she'd accomplished at last. For a moment I thought I could take her by the hand, now that her agony was over, and she would sit up and smile with triumphant fatigue—as if she'd just struggled mightily to give birth, or as if we had been waiting merely for a fever to break, or as if we'd been waiting with impatience for an hourglass to run out so we could turn it over again. I remember hearing the buzz and click of the clock radio on her nightstand, then the sound of the next minute falling into place, and for that one moment, I was as shocked by her death as I would have been had she been healthy and died in an accident or inexplicably in her sleep.

My father left the small room with his sister's arm around him, and I remained behind, alone with my mother, with her body. I spoke into her ear, carefully. Is it merely a superstition that hearing is the last of the senses to fade? I could almost hear her voice: "Nobody can say it's not true" and I could almost see the way she would raise her eyebrows, purse her lips, and hold up an admonitory finger. So I spoke.

"I love you, Mom. Go now. Don't be afraid."

After a moment's hesitation, I added, "Go on ahead. I'll see you later."

Nobody can say it's not true.

My father came in. He looked at her and turned away. It seemed reflexive, like pulling your hand back from a flame or shielding your eyes from the sun. He asked me to step out to the living room.

"The people from the Becker will be here soon," he said. "Do me a favor. Your mother still has her oxygen hose on. And that catheter thing. I don't want them going in there and . . ." He stopped, collecting himself, and took out a handkerchief and blew his nose. Gently, his hand on my upper arm, he turned me back to the small room.

After I had done what he asked, I went into the kitchen and poured myself a tumbler of whiskey.

"Dickie? Go easy with that, will you?" Aunt Kitty said.

"What? What are you talking about?"

"Never mind. Just go easy, that's all."

By the time the funeral director and his two assistants arrived, I was working on a second tumbler. I walked unsteadily to the door and opened it. A large man in a dark coat held out his hand, and when I tried to shake it he grasped my fingers. He was wearing an ill-fitting hairpiece, and I disliked him immensely for it; it seemed a vain discomfort with mortality, unseemly, an affront. Behind him on the porch, two men flanked a stretcher, looking down. A stretcher? Truly drunk by now, I wanted to spit at them, "You're too late!"

"Come in. Come in," my father said from behind me, and I took a step back and let them file past me.

My father and the funeral director went into the kitchen. The other two men carried the stretcher into the makeshift room. I sat in a chair, glowering into my drink, and silently indulged myself in all the impotent rage I felt. I wanted to bellow, "I know who you are!" to the three men in the black coats. "Get out of here! Get out of this house!" They were *they*. *They* who had found my mother too Dutchified, too citified, too rude, too poor, too human. Who had patronized her and threatened her with ridicule every day of her life. Who had determined her babies didn't need her breasts, who sold her powdered formula instead and a steam machine to sterilize bottles, while her breasts, ignored, ached with their uselessness. Who crossed her heart instead and lifted her breasts a certain way beneath a certain kind of sweater. Who called her illegitimate, a broad, a bitch. Who sold her poison smoke with coupons on each pack to save for cheap household appliances. Who determined what she did and did not deserve. Who convinced her *they* knew how to live but would tell her only how not to. Of course they would look like this officious black-clad trinity, their eyes averted, come to remove the offending object of her body. I knew who they were. I took another angry drink.

The funeral director came in from the kitchen, and I heard, from the small room, the metallic noise of the stretcher on its folding X's as they adjusted it, and the locking of restraining belts. He opened the door. I smoldered deep in the chair; my father stayed in the kitchen. The two men pushed the stretcher from the small room to the front door, stopped, and lifted it. And they carried my mother's body from my father's house.

chapter sixteen

1990

I RANG THE bell. My father opened the door.

"Good to see you! How was your trip?"

He opened his arms to hug me. The black bag slung over my shoulder excused my awkward, back-patting response. Nevertheless, my resolve began to bleed from me. What was I doing? I felt like an assassin.

"I got turned around," I said. "I almost didn't get here."

"What do you mean?"

"I missed the exit for 22 and ended up over on South Mountain."

"Oh yeah. It's all different now. I probably should have warned you. Come in. Sit down. How are you?"

"First I've got to take a leak," I said and headed for the small bathroom off the back porch.

I could feel a familiar, debilitating melancholy coming over me, related in some way to the smells of that old house, mildew and sweat and smoke and stale beer. The smells of childhood, all the way back to when this was my grandfather's house: Pappy Hoffman sitting in his chair in the living room with his cane hooked over the arm, a dead cigar in a heavy glass ashtray, a blue coffee can—"Good to the Last Drop"—next to his chair for a spittoon, tall brown bottles of beer. Mommom in the kitchen: boiled potatoes and onions, pork roast and sauerkraut.

I was shrinking. Sitting on the toilet with the seat down, I felt a split-second shock that my feet reached the floor. After a while I stood up, turned around to flush the toilet as alibi for my privacy, decided not to, and returned to the living room.

My father was in his favorite chair. He gestured toward the sofa. "So," he said. "Sit down. Sit down and tell me about your life."

"Dad," I said. I began to tremble. I hadn't been home, to Allentown, since shortly after my mother died, more than five years earlier. My father had come to Boston a couple of times, once at Christmas, and again when my daughter, Veronica, was born, and I had called him, dutifully, every three weeks or so, "Just checking in. How are you? Good. We're fine. Take care." Now I was here with difficult and painful things to say to him, and he was smiling, glad to see me. The last thing I wanted was to sucker-punch him.

"Dad," I said again. My throat closed.

He frowned. "Sit down. Sit down."

I took a deep breath. Although I'd staged this meeting, I had also taken care not to rehearse it. That seemed pointless and one-sided and vaguely cowardly. At one point I had thought to write him a long, careful letter, like Kafka's to his father, but I was a writer and he was uncomfortable with scribbling even a brief note, so that seemed unfair. Besides, though I told myself I had no expectations, deeper down I was hoping for something; I wanted not only to be heard, I wanted things to change between us. The telephone was out of the question. I sat on the sofa and unzipped the black bag.

I took out a picture of myself at eight and placed it on the coffee table between us. I didn't know how to begin. I reached in the bag again and took out three bronze medallions, one for each year I'd been sober in Alcoholics Anonymous. I reached across the table and held them out to him; they clinked as he turned them over, examining them.

"Do you know what those are?" I asked him.

"No. Well. I guess I have some idea."

"Those are the medals I won in the war, Dad."

"What war?"

"The war, Dad. My war. Let me tell you about my war."

I had reviewed dozens of ways to begin this conversation. Now I chose one.

On the day I graduated from college, my father took me aside and gave me an envelope with five new hundred-dollar bills in it. I began to open it, but he put his hand over mine and said, "Just put that in your pocket." He looked around furtively as if this were a top-secret transaction. He took me by the elbow and turned me to walk a little farther away from my mother, my brother Joe, my aunt Kitty, and Mammy Etta. "I'm walking along over there, and this guy with a beard comes up to me and says, 'You must be Mr. Hoffman. You know you should be very proud.' And then he says, 'I mean considering all he's been through.' So I thanked him. But what the hell, I'm thinking. This professor or whoever he is knows more about my kid than I do. I feel like I've lost track of you. We should talk. Sometime."

"Sure," I said. I had half a hit of acid in me. I'd just smoked some blond hash tucked inside a Marlboro. I was stoned.

It was a good place to start. I asked if he remembered that conversation. He nodded. "Well it's time we had that talk," I said. "I need to get some things squared away. I need to set the record straight. I've fucked up a lot of things in my life and almost killed myself a couple of times. I'm trying to get myself squared away for my kids, so they won't have to go through what I went through. I've kept a lot of this from you. Mostly I never told you how angry I am at you."

The anger was kicking in as I spoke, and the anger released me from the need to protect him from the truth. His face began to redden.

"I've come to understand a lot about myself, Dad, the drinking, the drugs, the ways I've gotten twisted up. I want to talk about what it was like growing up here. The stuff that happened to me. I'm angry at you because you beat the shit out of me when I was a kid, and it hurt me, Dad, it really fucked me up. You need to know that. I need you to know that."

It was hard to see the pain on his face. I'd been sweating and shaking; now I was crying. When I needed to, I glanced at the picture of my boyhood self on the coffee table; otherwise I cried and looked at his red and stricken face. It is inescapable: my love for my family—the real love, not the illusion I professed—is sibling to anger and grief.

By displacing one and trying to elude the other, I had stayed naive and grotesquely childish.

"You can't say I didn't love you," he said.

"I didn't. I didn't say you didn't love me. I said you beat the shit out of me."

"I spanked you; yes, of course I did. That's what we did in those days."

"No." I refused to argue the point.

"No what?"

In my black bag I'd brought a slotted spatula like the one he used to use on my bare behind. From time to time when I'd been tempted to make excuses for him, I would look at it, hold it in my hand, wonder what could possess a man to hit a child with this thing. The "potato-turner" is what he called it. I took it out and held it up between us. "You never hit me with one of these things, right? You never hit me with one of these?"

"I don't know. I don't remember. I believe I probably threatened you with it once or twice."

"You hit me with it, Dad. And more than once or twice, god damn it. I used to have raw welts on my ass from it. What were you thinking? What the fuck were you thinking? I mean I try to imagine it, Dad, but I could no more pull down Robert's pants and hit his soft little ass with a thing like this than I could fly to the fuckin' moon. What was going on in your head?"

He was looking away, his mouth hanging open, tears rolling down his face.

"I have more to say, Dad. I didn't come here to hurt you. Thirty years ago I stopped telling you the truth. I couldn't. Now I have to, and it hurts like hell, but I have to tell it and you have to listen. Because you were right: you did lose track of me, only it was a lot earlier than you thought." I felt like I was going too fast. I didn't want to tell him about Tom yet. "I have to tell you because I don't want to be afraid of you anymore."

"Afraid?" He looked astonished. "What did I do to you? Why would you be afraid of me? I'm your father."

I stood up, unbuckled my belt, drew it through my belt loops, and doubled it. I lay it on the table next to the picture, the medallions, and the spatula. I sat down quietly and stared at the table. Tears came. I took a deep breath. I was still afraid of him. I wanted to drop the whole thing. I wished I'd never come. I needed to settle down. I didn't want my voice to quake or squeak.

"What?"

That single syllable enraged me. Once again I felt my life diminished by his unwillingness to remember, his passivity, his defeat. I had a dream once in which my father was having surgery. When the surgeon opened his massive belly with a long incision from groin to chin, my mother, my brother Mike, and my brother Bob stepped out.

I shook the belt at him. "You terrorized us," I said. "There's no other word for it. You used to come home from work, from the fuckin' brewery, drunk, I guess, and beat the shit out of me and Bob. I remember screaming and running to get away from you, the two of us on our hands and knees while you swung your belt at us. So don't give me any of this shit about 'spankings.' I was scared to death of you."

"How can that be? I remember playing catch with you in the yard when I came home from work. Of course Bob was too sick. But you and I. When I coached the American

Legion team, you went along to every game. You were the batboy! How come you don't remember that?"

"Who says I don't remember that?"

"Well you talk as if . . . never mind."

"No, go ahead, say it. There were good times too. But I'm not talking about good times versus bad times, Dad. I'm talking about assault and battery on a child. What if I knew a kid in my classroom was getting whipped with a belt or a metal spatula? I'd have to file a child-abuse report. You must know that, after all the years you worked with kids. I loved being batboy on that team! That's just not what I came to talk about. What about you? Do you remember only the good times? Do you remember any of this stuff I'm talking about?"

"What about Bob?" He was wiping away tears when his face contorted and a stuck cry squeaked in his throat. "Was he afraid of me too? He must have been afraid of me too."

"I'm not here to speak for Bob. Sometime I want to talk *about* him though. In this house people die and—poof!—they're gone. We have a funeral, then no one ever mentions them again. We don't tell stories about them. We don't laugh about funny things they once did. We don't remember things they used to say. We just forget them. They vanish."

"Your mother was the one."

"What do you mean?"

"Your mother was the one who remembered everything." He put his head down and shielded his eyes with his hand. His body quaked as he wept, quietly. After a while, he took his hand from his brow, looked at me for a second, and turned away. "I know you think I don't still grieve for those two boys." He touched the lampshade next to him with his fingertips. "Your brother Joe is pissed off at me for that too. I want you to know I try sometimes, but I can't help it, Dick, I hardly remember either of those two boys. Sometimes I lie awake at night and try, and all I can remember is burying them. It hurts like hell. It's what? Five years now your mother's gone? She was the one who was able to remember.

"I try. A few weeks after your mother died, I got out our wedding pictures and I stood one up on the mantle over there. And a couple of pictures of your brothers. I even put some flowers around. Then one day somebody walks in and says, 'Christ, it looks like a god-damned mortuary in here.' So I threw out the flowers, put the pictures back in the drawer upstairs. Look at this place!" He gestured with his hand. "It looks like a fuckin' motel, like nobody ever lived here."

"Who?" I asked him. "Who said such a stupid thing?"

He waved his hand in front of his face, brushing away the question. I wondered how we had digressed so far. I was wary of him. His grief was real, but so was mine, and my anger, and my outrage. Was he hiding, depending on the pity I felt for him? I felt invited to lay aside my wrath and embrace him and cry with him.

I looked at the photograph of the boy whose story I had come here to tell, and I knew, in that moment, that all unspoken truths do not comprise one silence, all losses do not merge into a single grief, all injuries do not add up to one great wound. I was not willing to settle for a mass grave with a single marker. Besides, one of those buried in the rubble was still alive.

"What about *this* boy?" I said quietly, taking the picture

from the table and holding it out to him. "Do you remember him?"

He took the photograph and looked at it for a long moment and with such a growing tenderness on his face that I looked away, feeling like an intruder. He placed the picture facedown on his chest, resting the frame on the sill of his big round belly. "Seems like we remember him different," he said. "Seems like we remember a lot of things different."

IT WAS 1983. My son had just been born. My mother was dying. I was determined to write my novel and quit drinking. It had been two days since my last drink, and I was pretty shaky.

Once when I was batboy on my father's baseball team, I wandered too near a player swinging a weighted bat in the on-deck circle; I heard my father shout, "Look out!" and when the bat hit the back of my skull there was a flash of white light as I lost consciousness. I saw or felt—or was—that flash of light for an instant some thirty years later while I was writing. The next thing I remember I was on the floor, coming to, my wife asking me if I was all right.

I had been writing a series of sketches I hoped would serve as fodder for a novel about a working-class Catholic boy from Cooperstown, New York, who dreamed of being the first American Pope to be elected to the Baseball Hall of Fame. It was to be, by turns, lyrical, satirical, and elegiac. So I went foraging among my memories for incidents, places, people to shape to the story's purposes.

Later that evening, after dinner, still feeling weak and shaky, I sat down at my typewriter and rolled up the page to see what I'd written. I'd been making a list. The last item read: "Baseball coaches: Dad, Tom Feifel."

The popular view of withdrawal is that all sorts of phantoms, monsters, spacemen, and surreal distortions assault the alcoholic and that they are mere chimeras to be withstood until the detox is complete. For me, however, the demons were real. It was as if alcoholism were fighting back, and the Marquis of Queensberry be damned. The booze seemed to say, "Oh yeah? You don't need me anymore? Fine. Then let's see you handle this. Remember?" Wham! White light.

I drank all night. I remember lying on the floor, stoned, looking up at scene after scene of my life on the ceiling, a Sistine arrangement of panels my attention brought to cinematic life. And in the central panel an impostor father, mounted on a young boy, thrusts and moans, while off to the side a figure I recognize, my father, stands like a Picasso harlequin, unmoving, his countenance blank.

It wasn't as if I had ever completely forgotten Tom. I'd never denied the events; instead, I'd insisted on their unimportance. It was one bad year, I told myself. I'd shaken it off like a batter hit by a pitch who grits his teeth and trots to first base to applause.

I drank for three more years, sick drinking, around the clock, sneaking, hiding, ashamed, seeking an oblivion just short of suicide.

RECENTLY I WAS at a Little League game with my son, Robert, when I saw him staring at a boy who had been horribly burned, his face a mass of scar. I touched Robert on the shoulder to break the spell. He whispered, "Dad, what's the matter with that kid?" I explained that he was in a fire, that he'd been burned. My eyes welled and I trembled. It wasn't so much pity for the boy that moved me, although I pitied him, but my identification with him. And what if that disfiguring blaze burned all the pictures too? Who can describe that boy? Whose memory can be trusted now except my own, slow as it is to recall, reluctant as it is to reveal its tracings?

"MEMORY IS TRICKY, Dad. Sometimes you have to forget. To go on. I know that. But other times, to go on, you have to remember."

"You lost me," he said.

I was going too fast. He'd been lost in thought and hadn't heard what I said. He held the picture at arm's length, put on his glasses, and looked at it for a moment.

"I have some very good memories of this boy," he said.

"I do too," I said, and held out my hand for the picture. He gave it to me with one hand, took off his glasses with the other. "I do too," I said again. I lay the photograph flat on the table next to the belt, the medallions, and the spatula. "And I have some memories that damn near killed me."

It was time to tell him about Tom, but I didn't know how to begin. Several years before, during one of my mother's hospitalizations, I'd gotten drunk and told my brother Joe what had happened. At the time, I believed that if I could prevent Tom from molesting another kid, I would be able to finish with it and, my adult duty discharged, get on with my life. I went to see a detective in the police department, someone my brother knew, and told her the story. I also wrote an anonymous letter to the director of the Downtown Youth Center, telling what had happened.

"There are things that happened to me when I was a kid that you don't know about," I said to my father. "At least I don't think you do. Things I blame you for, that I'm angry about to this day. Tell me: what does the name Tom Feifel mean to you?"

His face reddened; he frowned, lowered his head, brought his fingertips to the bridge of his nose. "He used to run the North End, no, the Downtown Youth Center. That's it. He coached you when you played on that football team—what was it? The Bears. And you played baseball for him too, at Jordan Park." He looked up as if to ask "Right?," as if he'd performed an extraordinary feat.

I was suddenly too angry to speak. The last time I'd been here, I'd asked about Tom during a commercial while we were watching a ball game. "What do you hear about Tom Feifel? Remember him? Is he still coaching?" I wanted to know if the interview and my letter had made any difference.

"Oh, he's still coaching, I guess," my father had answered. "Still coaching and fuckin' around with little boys."

I watched the rest of the ball game in silence, staggered by his reply. Was he telling me he knew? Or that he knew about Tom but assumed I was never involved? Did that mean he didn't care if someone else's kid was molested? Did he think it was no big deal? Did he condone it? I remember feeling as incorporeal and abstracted as I'd ever been when Tom was violating me, and struggling to control my quivering insides. Now, five years later, he seemed to remember nothing more than the fact that Tom had been my coach.

I asked him if he remembered making the remark. "I

believe you," he said. "I don't remember saying that, but I believe you."

"I don't remember. I don't remember. What the hell did you mean, 'still fuckin' around with little boys'? Do you have any idea?" I was on my feet now, fists clenched at my sides, leaning over him, roaring. "DO YOU HAVE ANY FUCKING IDEA WHAT HAPPENS TO A LITTLE BOY'S SOUL WHEN YOU SHOVE A COCK UP HIS ASS? DO YOU?"

His face contorted with understanding as I stood over him, teeth gritted, crying hard, and I resisted the impulse to look away from the horror on his face. He gasped, sobbed, covered his face with his hands. I turned and reached in the black bag for an account I'd written of Tom's abuse. "Read this," I said, and put it in his hand.

I walked to the front window and looked out at the street. The window was covered with my mother's plants: dieffenbachia, philodendron, aloe, wandering Jew, begonia, crown of thorns. It struck me that my father had been caring for her plants for these past years, that the coleus and saxifrage on saucers on the air conditioner were the only shrine to her memory he allowed himself, and I suddenly felt I had made a terrible mistake. I wanted to yell "Wait!," run across the room, and snatch the pages from his hands.

I looked up at the leaded stained glass at the top of the window. I was shaking as if I were freezing or detoxifying, but I needed to hold my ground until my father finished reading. As I stared at the frosted panels that looked like ice holding thousands of tiny bubbles, I thought of my mother. Her belief that we would all be reunited must have been impressed on me more deeply than I'd ever known, or maybe what I felt then had to do with a boyhood need for her comfort; anyway, I knew she was witnessing this day. As I stood there, on the exact spot where she died, I envisioned my father joining her some day in the future, and I heard her tell him, "Of course I was there. You did just fine." And she assured him, as she had assured me countless times, "He loves you, you know. You did just fine. You both did just fine." This weird daydream assured me that my father and I would come through this ordeal together, which was in fact the very guarantee I'd needed as a child: that no matter how shamed and filthy I believed I was, despite what Tom had taught me, my parents would never abandon me. My rage, devoid of that old fear, contracted to a mix of anger and resolve. A grown man now, what I needed was clarity. I needed some answers. Behind me my father moaned.

I returned to the sofa and waited. He sat with his head down and his arms crossed on top of his big belly, the pages I'd given him rolled in one hand, quaking now and again with a stifled sob. It was a long time before he spoke.

"We'll find him, the cocksucker, and make him pay," he said. "I wish I'd known about this back then. But now that you finally told me, I'll get him, the son of a bitch. I know a few guys who can find him. Don't worry, we'll get him." He wiped tears from the corners of his eyes.

I wanted to throw myself on him then and cry, as I wish I could have long ago, but I still held him responsible for Tom's abuse in ways I needed to talk about.

"No. It's not your battle anymore, Dad; it's mine now."

"It's not just yours. You're not the only one with a score to settle with him now. Since your mother died, since I retired, I've been trying to make my peace with the man upstairs." He jabbed the rolled pages upward. "And I thought I had accounts pretty well squared away." He sighed. "This changes everything."

"Hold it," I said.

"Well what did you think? You were going to tell me about this and I was going to just sit here? I'm going to do now what I would have done back then if you had told me. I mean it. We're going to get the son of a bitch."

"Dad."

"There's ways of dealing with cocksuckers like that. There's a couple of guys in my poker game who'll know where to find him."

"Dad. Dad hold it. Please, god damn it!"

"What?"

I was crying, but I felt no connection to it; it was like cutting onions. I was intent on the questions I needed to ask him.

"What about you?"

"What about me? What do you mean, what about me?"

"What did you mean when you said that about Tom, that he was still fucking around with little boys?"

"That he was, you know"—he sneered—"queer. A faggot."

"There. Ah, there it is. That sneer of yours. That fucking sneer was why I couldn't tell you. Don't you see? That sneer locked me in Tom's bedroom like you nailed the fucking door shut!"

He shook his head as if he were about to speak.

"No, Dad, you listen now. I want to set a few things straight." I was pointing at him. "First of all, whether

Tom was gay or not has nothing to do with it. He was a child molester, a rapist." My father shifted in his chair as if it was hard for him not to argue. "What if I'd been your daughter? Not your son, your daughter. Would that have been okay?

"But just for the record, I don't think that Tom was gay. His whole pornography collection—and I saw enough of it to know—was straight." I stopped so he would look at me. "It was just like yours, Dad. That's another thing I want to know about sometime. The bathroom closet. Did you think I wouldn't find that shit? Did you want me to?

"And now you want to go after Tom. But what are you so angry about? That he fucked me? That he made me suck his cock? What if he'd only beat me like you did?"

He was staring straight ahead, unblinking, tears streaming from his eyes, rolling the pages into a tight scroll. "I always knew I was fucked up," he said, "but I never knew I was this fucked up." He put the rolled pages on the coffee table, where they loosened and swelled, and he wiped his cheeks dry with his palms. "If this could happen to you and you were too afraid of your dad to come to him and ask for help,"—and here he cried out—"then my whole fuckin' life has been a waste!"

"Don't!" I said. I'd been afraid of this. For a long time I'd convinced myself that telling him the truth would kill him or that he would take his own life. Although I'd come to recognize this as an excuse for my own frightened silence, I also knew that his capacity for self-hatred was real.

"Don't trash it all. Do you hear me? I've been careful not to do that. Damn it, you be careful too. You want white hats on the good guys and black hats on the bad guys, go to the movies. You took care of two sick kids for years in this house. You worked like a horse. You stuck it out, and you did a lot of things right. Don't think for a minute I've forgotten any of that. This bullshit—'my whole fuckin' life has been a waste'—is a cop-out, Dad. I didn't come here for that."

"What *did* you come here for?" he roared at me. "Tell me! What the hell did you come here for? You're telling me stuff that happened thirty years ago."

"No!" I bellowed back at him. "I'm telling you what's been happening to me for thirty years. I'm trying to stop it, the rage and the shame and the hating myself."

"But what the hell do you want from me now? I'm angry enough to kill this bastard and you tell me it's none of my god-damned business, that I can't do nothing about it anymore, and when I agree with you, and when I tell you how I feel, you get pissed off at me and tell me it's a cop-out. Tell me what you want from me!"

His question overwhelmed me. Suddenly, I wanted everything I had ever wanted from him and all at once. I wanted him to hold and comfort me. I wanted him to tell me he was proud of me. I wanted him to undo everything that was wrong, fix everything that was broken, explain everything that was unclear. I glanced at the picture of my boyhood self, with his clip-on bow tie and suspenders, and I spilled forward, my elbows on my knees, my head in my hands, and wept furiously.

When I straightened and looked at my father, I saw an old man with his eyes red from crying, at a loss, unsure what to do, and I recognized him, not "Dad," but the man himself, as I had on only a few occasions before, always between a death and a burial.

"This is what I wanted," I said, "to tell the truth for a change. To talk to you."

FOR THE NEXT three days we talked. Sometimes we walked the dog or watched a ball game on TV or drove somewhere in the car, but all the time we talked. It was hard work, and there was a rhythm to it. Like building something—or dismantling something, for that matter—the work defined the pace, the balance between activity and rest, progress and repose. I first noticed this soon after I'd decided to stay, although at first I misunderstood it.

"I'd better get my stuff from the car," I said.

"When do you have to head back?"

He asked the question in what I took to be the language of obligation.

"I should leave Sunday morning." I sighed, thinking I was matching my idiom to his. "I don't need to be back at work until Tuesday, but I should probably get back a day early and give Kathi a break. Spend some time with the kids." I heaved myself up from the sofa, sighed, and looked at the clock. I'd been there forty minutes.

I stepped out into the glare of the afternoon. Trees used to line our street until the Power & Light Company cut them all down. Now the porches of all the houses on the block are useless for most of the day. Taking my suitcase from the trunk of the hot car, I remembered my mother's story about the man with the clipboard who came to the door one day, dressed in gray Dickies and wearing a cap with a lightning bolt on it. He told her he was almost through gathering signatures from the neighbors to allow PP&L to remove any obstructions to the new power lines they planned to put up. He went on to explain that with upgraded electrical service the homes would retain their value no matter what unforeseen trends threatened to devalue properties in the surrounding neighborhoods. Having played on her fears that black or foreign-born people were about to weaken the only investment my parents had, he handed her the pen and she signed. Later that same week, when they came to cut down the maple that shaded the front of the house, my mother asked them what they thought they were doing and they showed her her signature on the paper. "I'm such a moron," she said.

When I lugged my suitcase into the house, my father was watching a ball game on TV. I was stunned. Did he think that we'd had our catharsis, that now we'd sit around and watch the Phillies or the Yankees or the Sox for the next three days? I made a big deal of putting down my bag, squatting with my back to him and to a beer commercial, as if I was looking for something. While I tore through socks, underwear, pajamas, slacks, I tried to understand what was going on. I felt insulted, dismissed. I stole a look at him, and in just that instant he blinked, a tear rolled down his cheek, and he flicked it away quickly the way you would shoo a fly. And I understood. I remembered.

Television sports had been the hearth my family gathered around for almost as long as I could remember. Before the days of cable TV and remote control, we had three televisions stacked in a pyramid in the corner, with three ball games going on at once. I remembered Bob hunched over his score book, sometimes with a radio earphone on, watching his game with the sound turned off, while we watched two other games, with me sitting close to turn the sound up on one set and down on the other. I remember

Mel Allen's voice, broadcasting for the Yankees. "So look for the three-ring sign," I could still hear him say, "and remember: nothing goes together like baseball and Ballantine." And the jingle for Gillette Blue Blades: "LOOK sharp—ta da da da da, and BE sharp, ta da da da da!" To so totally immerse ourselves in the games, the lore, the statistics, the particulars and personalities had been, for all those frightening years, our common comfort. My father was asking for a time-out.

I closed the suitcase and put it by the coat closet near his chair. The game had resumed, and I stood behind him pretending to watch it. When I rested my hand on his shoulder, he reached up, eyes still on the television, and covered it with his. "We'll talk some more," he said.

"When do you have to head back?" he had asked, and I had only partly understood the question. What he wanted to know was, *How long do we have to do this job?*

"You find what you were looking for?" he asked me.

"Yes," I said, and bent and kissed him on the top of his head.

THE LIES THAT had estranged us from each other were not conscious ones; they were made of shame and silence and fear, and blame was irrelevant. Our tasks were different. Mine was to shed the props and poses I'd found necessary to come this far, not only the black bag of talismans that insisted I'd been wronged, but the handful of postures—the good son, the college-educated-but-never-forgot-his-roots son, the always-there-in-a-pinch son, the father-of-the-grandchildren son, the healthy you-don't-need-to-worry-about-me son, and others—that had defined me to him for so many years. His task, I imagine, was to muster the courage to face who he'd sometimes been as a young father, without going on to condemn himself on the one hand nor rationalize his behavior on the other. What we were building together as we walked his dog through Jordan Park, as we visited the family plot at the cemetery, as we sat in our stocking feet and watched a ball game on TV, was trust.

On one of our walks I asked him about the other men I remembered from boyhood. They were peripheral but vaguely exemplary: the men at the barbershop, the old prizefighter who ran the newsstand, the white-haired Irishman, sober by then, who ran the youth center and who had drunk himself out of professional baseball. As we talked I could see their faces: the boxer with his flattened nose, one eye half-shut and wandering; the ruddy-faced, bald, mustached man who I remembered sometimes helped my father lift my brothers in or out of the car.

"That would have been Johnny Kovach," he said. "Nice guy, he was. He died, hell, I guess it was back when you were a kid." He stopped walking; at first I thought he was looking at something. The dog nuzzled his leg, whimpering, and whacked my knee with his tail. My father pursed his lips and frowned and shook his head slightly. I wanted to pick up a stick and throw it to be rid of the dog, but I thought my father was about to say something. He was still for a long time, looking down, and then he squeezed my shoulder once and we continued walking, resuming our game of fetch with the dog.

And I remembered a wet night sitting alone in my father's car outside a funeral parlor when I was twelve or thirteen. I was lost in a dream of romance, as I was much of the time then, thinking of a girl named Carol. I loved her chastely and desperately. I wanted to be a priest, but I'd been taught that only those whom God had chosen were so honored. Those who were chosen somehow knew beyond all doubt, and I was still uncertain, waiting for a sign. During those years, instead of biting my arm, I hid in an altar boy's feeling of holiness: the vestments, incense, candles, Latin, taken all together, were sometimes enough to suppress the lurid imagery that continued to intrude on my awareness. My fixation on Carol was self-defense. If God didn't choose me, there was still Carol, whom the nuns had chosen Queen of the May to represent the Virgin Mary. If Carol would have me, I might yet be saved. I sat in the dark car chewing my nails and thinking of how I would brush Carol's bangs aside and kiss her forehead, and show her how chaste I was and different from other boys.

The door opened and my father got behind the wheel. The light had come on for a moment when he opened the door, and I saw that in addition to being drenched, he was shaken. He put both his hands together on the steering wheel and rested his head on them. After a moment I reached over and put my hand on his shoulder, but he straightened up then, started the car, and we drove off without talking. I don't remember where we were going.

We seemed to spend a lot of time in our separate pasts, with our separate griefs, as we walked side by side taking turns throwing sticks to the dog. The baseball field where I'd been shamed and humiliated was flooded and entirely under water, and I felt some delight at this without giving it much thought. When my father spoke again, I was surprised that he was still thinking of his friend.

"You were probably too young to remember him," he

said, heaving a good-sized stick into the water. The creek was high; the weeping willows trailed downstream in the clay-colored current. The dog plunged in without hesitating and, swimming with the current, gained on his prize.

"He was the kind of friend . . . You always want to have a friend like that. I remember his burial. Did I ever tell you about this? It was a shock if you weren't expecting it. The coffin's sitting there over the hole on those canvas straps, you know. Then the priest walks around sprinkling the whole thing with holy water. So far so good. But all of a sudden he throws a shovelful of dirt on the casket. Dirt! Rocks! Boom, just like that. It shook me up. He was Hungarian, Johnny, and that's what they do, I guess. But up to then it was nothing out of the ordinary. None of the Hunkies thought nothing of it, but now I'm worried we're going to have to stay and watch them lower the box and fill up the hole and I couldn't take that. I never seen anything like it really. It seems like a horrible custom. Maybe if I was expecting it. It don't give much comfort to the people who are left behind."

We watched the dog take the stick in his teeth and turn, or try to; it was all he could do to keep his head above the water.

I was thinking of what my father said, especially the word *dirt*. Earth, I thought, not dirt. I was struck by how strange and right it seemed that we use the same word for a trowel of it or the whole of it.

The dog paddled harder and harder, swept downstream, until my father and I seemed to become alarmed at the same moment.

"Damn stupid dog!" my father muttered. "Look at him."

I began to make my way along the soggy bank as best I could.

"Let go of the god-damned stick, you dumb dog!" my father shouted. "Let go of the stick!"

I was trying to run now, slipping and sliding in the wet, spongy grass. Just as the creek began to bend, and he would have disappeared from view, he let go of the stick and struggled across the current until, after two or three tired attempts, he managed to climb onto the bank.

When I got to him, he was retching and coughing, and as I squatted down to pet him, my father called, "Come here, boy. Come on, boy. Come on." The dog straightened, shook himself all over, sneezed, and trotted off to its master.

When I rejoined them, my father was on his knees with his arms around the panting wet animal. "If I lost this dog, I don't know what I'd do," he said, while the dog nuzzled and licked him and he thumped its side. "I don't know what I'd do." He attached the leash to the dog's collar.

And then he stood up, his face streaked with mud, and stared into the distance as if he were listening for something. After a long moment's reverie he turned to me and said, "What do you say we head up to the cemetery for a while?"

THE DOG TURNED around and around in the back seat, smearing the windows with its wet tail, considering how to make itself comfortable. My father started the car, released the brake, and stepped on the gas before I'd even shut my door. The dog lurched, regained its footing, then curled itself on the folded blanket and snorted. My father drove as if his fresh tears were something he'd just remembered to tell my mother or one of my brothers and he was worried he might forget. He gunned the engine, ran the yellow lights, peeled rubber on turns. We rode with our elbows out the windows, and neither of us spoke until we turned at the break in the stone wall onto the gravel cemetery road.

"Let's head up this way first," he said, turning sharply to the right. We were going too fast and fishtailed a little on the gravel.

"Your grandparents are buried up here, near your uncle Francis's first wife, Flo." I knew this of course. We skidded and stopped.

"Roll up your window partway so the dog don't get out and shit all over the place," he said, rolling his halfway as example. Then he slammed the door and walked quickly down the row of headstones to his parents' graves as if he were late for an appointment.

Although he hadn't said so, I knew he wanted to be alone. I leaned against the car, surprised we had stopped here first; usually we paid a brief visit to this part of the cemetery just before we left to go home.

EARLIER, OVER MORNING coffee, we'd talked about my grandparents. I remembered that when Bob and I were little we asked Dad about the brown necklace of scar around Mommom's throat.

"I guess they just opened her up like this," Dad told us gesturing with his finger from ear to ear. "And they tipped back her head, took the bad thing out, and sewed her back up again."

"What was in her throat?" Bob asked. "Did she get a frog in her throat?"

"She had a goiter in her throat."

"Stupid," I said to Bob. We had already discussed this. A goiter, I had informed him, was a kind of cross between a worm and a snake.

When we visited we seldom got farther than the vestibule before Mommom would give us each an apple. I remember Bob biting his while Dad was still tugging off his other coat sleeve. My grandmother believed in apples. Apples on arriving, and one piece of hard candy each when our coats were back on to go home.

And, according to my father, she also believed in whippings, with belts, hairbrushes, coat hangers, and spatulas.

"But I always knew she loved me," he said. "I always deserved it. Pappy couldn't whip me after his accident, so it was up to my mother to keep me out of trouble."

"He fell from a ladder?"

"From a scaffold. It damn near killed him. Killed his partner. Pappy landed on his feet and shattered them and drove his leg bones right up through his hips. His partner landed on his back on the brick pile. Pappy was in the hospital for a long time before we were even sure he'd live."

"Was he compensated? Did they give him some kind of disability pension or something? He worked over at Mack, right?"

"That's right. Well, they ended up taking care of him pretty good. After he got out of the hospital, he had to show up for work at eight o'clock every morning to blow the whistle. That became his job. He blew the whistle in the morning, and then at lunchtime, and again at quitting. It may have been Pappy's fault, or his partner's. I don't know. I think my mother blamed it on the dead guy.

Nobody will ever know for sure. The scaffold was one of those you hook over the top of the wall and they didn't secure it right, and the damn thing just dumped them. They must have been about three stories off the ground. He was never the same after that. Well, you remember he always walked with a cane. Mostly after that he sat around and drank beer, I guess."

"And chewed tobacco I remember. He used to have his Maxwell House can right next to his chair."

"That's right."

"Bob and I used to make up stories about how he lost his finger. Was it his left hand or his right? His index finger was just a little stump."

"His left. He had an accident with a saw."

"One of us—I don't remember if it was me or Bob—came up with the idea that the Communists had chopped it off. I don't know why except that the nuns told us that's what the Indians did to Isaac Jogues and we just always made the Communists the bad guys. I remember it was blue."

"Oh, he had lousy circulation. He used to stick it in his coffee to warm it up. He had lousy circulation period; he smashed so many blood vessels in his legs and feet."

"I remember he always wore those high black shoes."

"And heavy socks. He could never keep his feet warm. He usually kept a little whiskey close by to warm him up. Of course he always liked his whiskey anyway. I never saw him drunk or anything like that, but I remember even back when he was still working, my mother would mix a raw egg in a double shot of brandy for him every morning for his breakfast."

"Hangover medicine."

"I don't know. My mother just said it was to get him going in the morning."

I kept quiet. The morning eye-opener and the severed finger and the deadly scaffold blunder were adding up in my mind. But the word "alcoholic" meant different things to each of us. To me it meant one who had become addicted to alcohol and whose life was skewed and distorted by that thirst and the need to hide it from others and oneself. I suspected that, to my father, even coming on the heels of my disclosure, it would ring with accusation and condemnation, and I had no such intention.

My father sighed. "When you were little, he used to slip me a few extra bucks once in a while to help out, but he didn't seem to want to have much to do with you kids. I don't know. I guess I never really had anything with my dad." He slowly shook his head and his eyes welled with tears. "No, I don't believe there was really anything between us. Like I said, it was really my mother who raised me. And my sister, Kitty."

THE DOG MANAGED to get its head through the narrow opening on the driver's side. It barked once, then panted with its tongue hanging out. I scratched the top of its head and watched my father until he moved his body a certain way, shifted his weight slightly, and I knew it was okay to join him.

The ground was wet and spongy. My father turned as I came up to him, and with his face flushed and his cheeks wet, he smiled. "I was remembering the bread store my mom and dad ran during the Depression." He shook his head. "I don't know why. Boy, I tell you I could almost smell that bread."

There was a pot of hyacinths, ragged from the storm, at the foot of the gravestone.

"Somebody's been here," I said.

"Kitty. She comes up here pretty regular. She always leaves some flowers and takes the dead ones away."

"Do Francie and Willy still have the greenhouse?"

"Well, Francie has it. Willy's dead. He died—it must be three, four years now. I didn't tell you that story? Come on, let's walk."

We picked our way over the soggy ground gingerly, a hand on each other's shoulder, at arm's length, steadying ourselves.

"I don't know what you remember about Willy. I think he was basically the guy that made the deliveries and Francie was the gardener, or florist, or whatever you want to call it. He always tried to be the tough guy, skinny little pisser that he was. So one day he's delivering some flowers to a house, or a potted plant or whatever the hell it was —it doesn't matter—and there's a carpenter or a painter or something, a colored guy, working in the doorway. So Willy tells the guy to move, and the guy says just a minute while I finish this, or something like that. And Willy—I guess you would call him a racist; he was always prejudiced—says something—I don't know—calls the guy a nigger, like 'Get out of my way, nigger,' and the guy gives him a push and Willy goes backward down the front steps and, boom, he has a heart attack, just like that."

We walked toward my mother and brothers' graves, away from the car, and the dog barked on and on.

"What happened to the other guy?"

"He went to jail. Manslaughter, I guess. Oh, Francie was going to kill him. Saying she was going to hire somebody to kill him. You couldn't talk sense to either of them, her nor Kitty. Nobody even knows what happened for sure. The other guy, the colored guy, was sorry. He was the one who called for the ambulance. It don't seem fair, but I guess a life was lost and they couldn't just let him go. Willy always was a big mouth. You talk like that to people long enough, eventually you get what you deserve."

We stopped beneath the great crucifix that rises from a rocky mound, planted with flowers, in the middle of the place.

"Will you listen to that god-damned dog," my father said.

"Should we go back and get him?"

"Argh! What for? He don't like being in the car, that's all. Come on; we're over here somewhere."

I hesitated.

"What's the matter?"

"Nothing." I was afraid. And surprised by my fear. What would happen when we stood by those graves together? What if he went to pieces now—could I care for him? And what if I broke down and fell apart in front of him—would I feel ashamed again? I didn't know whether I was more afraid of my father's grief or my own. I wished we hadn't stopped, because now I couldn't move my feet. My father was waiting. The dog was barking on and on.

"Here, give me your hand."

I did.

"Here. Over here it's not too wet. Step there. You see that spot? There. There you go. Now jump this swampy spot. Okay?"

I didn't believe for a moment that he thought I was worried about getting my feet wet. I jumped to the gravel road, and he let go of my hand.

"Thanks."

WE ALWAYS STAND beside the graves, or at the foot, and we walk around them as if the mounded earth had never settled or the torn sod healed. So I stood at the foot of the graves, and my father stood beside them with his head bowed. He appeared to be praying.

I was trying to feel my mother's presence. I figured that here at her grave I should be able to talk to her. From time to time since her death I had spoken to her, bringing her up to date about my life. It was more rhetoric than necromancy, like writing a letter to someone who you know will never read it. On occasion I had found myself talking to my brothers in the same way. I always spoke to Mike as if he were thirteen, his age when he died. When I spoke to Bob, he was in his late teens, the age I left him for New York, for college, and I always spoke of the places I'd been and things I'd seen just as I had during those years when, visiting home, I tried to bring back some of the world for him. Now I couldn't address them, and I felt empty.

"Room for one more here," my father said.

I didn't know what to say. I wasn't sure what he meant. There is space on the headstone for a fourth name, I thought; that must be it.

"That's my spot, right there," he said. "That's where you're to plant me, you hear? Right there. It's already paid for. I'll show you when we get home. The papers are in a special place, in a steel box, with the insurance stuff and my will and other things you'll need to take care of. I'll show you where it is when we get home. It's important you remember where it is. It's all taken care of ahead of time, so you shouldn't have any trouble when the time comes."

I felt annoyed. I had thought we'd come here to grieve together, and here he was, juggling self-pity with fatherly instructions. I knew the gray steel box he meant.

But I had also heard the sardonic note of the verb "plant," and, looking at his face, I suddenly heard, loud and clear, his desperate wish to be the next to die. It frightened me.

"What do you mean, 'when the time comes'?"

"Just what I said. Oh. No, no, no, relax. I'm feeling good. Oh, hell, I plan to be around another twenty-five or thirty years. No. Don't you worry. You and your brother will be cursing the old bastard for being such a stubborn son of a bitch." He took out a handkerchief, blew his nose, and smiled.

And I heard what he said, all of it, as if it were a prayer: that he should be buried here, that he should not die soon, and that Joe and I should survive him—that above all: that he should not have to bury another of his children.

"Nah," I said. "We'll give you another thirty years or so, but you stick around for too much longer after that and we might start cursing you."

He grinned. "Let me go get the dog before he pisses all over the car. I'll be back."

I watched him walk up the gravel road. It occurred to me that for years I had been talking to him the way I talk to the dead, conjuring an image of him that was both simple and paradoxical. It was as if he had died when I was ten, when I found myself unable to tell him about

Tom, and how ashamed and frightened I was, and I survived to piece together what would always remain, mostly, a ten-year-old's impressions. "I guess I never really had anything with my dad." He walked over the crest of the hill and after a few more moments the dog stopped barking.

IF I COULDN'T SPEAK to my mother, or to either of my brothers, even for my own sake, and if I didn't believe that they could answer me, what was I doing here? What does this mean? I asked myself. What does it mean that they have perished and I am standing here, their bodies under this ground? I had no idea.

Suddenly I had a memory, almost a sensation, of the feel of my brother Bob's shoulders, his arms and neck, when we were little, wrestling on our bedroom floor. For one split second I could feel the texture of his skin, the hair on the nape of his neck, and I cried out. In an instant all the perplexity that death had interposed between our bodies vanished, and I knew again that grief is desire. I squatted on my heels, leaning against the smooth back of a stranger's gravestone, and I let my body heave and sob and moan until it was done.

AT ONE POINT I went upstairs and found myself wandering from room to room, touching the walls and smelling the various familiar scents of the house as it came alive for me again. There was nothing very conscious about it, and I don't remember feeling good or bad or even nostalgic, but I had the sense that I was reacquainting myself with the place in an animal way.

I walked into the front bedroom. The dresser and the tall bureau were familiar, along with the matching night table next to my parents' bed. Above the bed the plaster was still chipped white where I'd removed the crucifix from the wall when my mother was dying; the crucifix itself lay flat on top of the bureau now, next to an upright photo sculpture of my father, eighteen or nineteen years old, in boots and combat fatigues, his parachutes on, front and back, smiling and giving the thumbs-up sign. He had sent the picture home before his unit went into combat. My grandmother had it fashioned into this two-dimensional copper-backed statue that she kept on a shelf in her dining room, the middle room downstairs, where I'd first seen it when I was a boy. Whenever we came here to visit, Bob and I asked to see it up close, and usually Mommom would take it down for us and let us handle it, always reminding us to be careful.

I was interested in the equipment. At the Army & Navy store Dad bought me a pair of combat boots to go along with the woven belt and the canteen that hooked in the brass eyelets of the belt so it would ride your hip the way the real G.I.s wore them, and the helmet liner with the leather chin strap I liked to suck on, but the boots were the wrong kind. Paratroopers couldn't wear such clunky brown boots, because you could foul your parachute on the buckles; instead, they wore high black boots that laced all the way to the top, and shined them daily "until you could see your face in them," my father said. I looked at the large pack on his back that contained the main parachute, and the smaller rolled emergency chute across his belly. I used to stare at this image and marvel at his courage. He was about to get on a plane that would drop him from the sky over enemies that would try to kill him even before he reached the ground, and he was grinning and giving the thumbs-up sign to the camera like a ballplayer stepping up to the plate.

Like other boys, I suspect, I thought of growing up only as getting bigger and stronger; I had no notion of myself as changing or developing. So my question was not whether one day I would have the courage to do something as heroic as my father had done during the war, but could I do it at all, or was I a coward? When I set my imagination to work on that question, all I could manage to feel, closing my eyes and falling through the sky, was terror. If my father had this courage, then maybe he could give it to me. So I asked him questions.

He had a yearbook, like a college yearbook, from the Army jump school, with his unit's insigne on the cover: Airborne Infantry, it said, above a maroon shield with a gold winged unicorn on it. The inside cover was a color picture of a bright blue sky filled with hundreds of white parachutes, brilliant in the sun. Like the shoulder patches, ribbons, paratrooper wings and other regalia he let me handle, the yearbook stirred me. I saw my father as a member of an elite. A lot of my questions, about equipment, procedures, situations, were really ways of trying to discover why he was so powerful and I was not.

"How come these guys have sneakers on?"

"You don't get your jump boots till after your first jump—that's your graduation; you get your wings and your boots."

"What if they give you a parachute that doesn't work?"

"If it doesn't work, it's your own damn fault. You pack your own chute. That's what those long tables are for." I was looking at a picture of an instructor showing his students how to fold the silk chutes, and tuck them into the pack. "The first jump, your jumpmaster packs your chute for you. After that you're on your own."

I figured I could never do that. Dad had made me a parachute for one of my green rubber infantrymen with a handkerchief and some string, and no matter how carefully I folded it, when I threw it up in the air, the soldier tangled in the string or the chute didn't open at all. I would probably ball it all up and kill myself.

"You're about as useful as a left-handed pisspot," he said to me sometimes when I was supposed to be helping him but didn't know what to do. I didn't understand the expression. On another occasion he asked me to steady a plank he was sawing, but I was too light to keep it from moving. He barked, "For Christ's sake, you're about as useful as a prick on a priest!" and by then I understood him only too well.

I had also seen paratroopers jumping from planes in the documentaries of World War II on television. Secretly I watched closely to see if Dad was in the movie. My imagination always seized on that moment when each successive paratrooper poised in the doorway until the jumpmaster slapped him on the shoulder.

"What if you got to the doorway and you were too scared to jump?"

"Then you got the jumpmaster's boot in your ass before you had a chance to shit your pants. That happened to a lot of guys."

I never asked him if it happened to him, although I must have wanted to.

"Did you really yell 'Geronimo!' when you jumped?"

"It don't make no difference what you yell; nobody can hear you anyway."

A KID WHO loved baseball, my father was taught to black his face and kill with his bare hands. He was thrown from a plane with a rifle, a bayonet strapped to his leg, and grenades on his chest. His eyes and ears alert with mortal terror, he hit, crumpled, rolled.

For all my questions, I never learned what happened to him. Once when I asked him if he had ever killed anyone, he said, "That's nothing to be proud of." During the war in Vietnam, while I was in college, he laughed at any talk of heroism. "You do what you need to survive and get home. All these fuckin' star-spangled assholes watched it through binoculars. They make me sick."

I imagined my father, schooled in fierceness, home from the war, marching under ticker tape and a blizzard of confetti, as I'd seen it on television over and over when I was a boy. I thought of him marching away from the slaughter with the others, in formation, empty rifles on their shoulders, just the way they'd hoped it would be, but hollow and hungover and mistaking, like all survivors, relief for pleasure, the absence of horror for peace, conventionality for safety. His dreams were gone, his memories buried. He raised his glass to the future. He married my mother. He went to work in the brewery.

Ashes. Amnesia. Anesthesia.

And rage.

NOW, FORTY-ONE YEARS OLD, I looked at the cut-out photo of a grinning nineteen-year-old paratrooper, and I noticed that he wore no helmet and carried no weapons.

He was not on his way to battle. He was having his picture taken. He was a son, not yet a soldier. And he was nobody's father. I looked a long time at his face, his eyes. This is the way he wanted his parents to see him and the way he wanted to be remembered if he didn't return.

It is the only picture of him in the house, propped up here on his bureau, in his bedroom's privacy. I wondered if he sat sometimes, right where I was sitting, and stared at it blankly, confounded as I am by the picture of myself at eight years old.

When my father was my age, forty-one, I was twenty, already a year older than he is in the picture, and only one year younger than he was when I was born. I thought of myself as a young man, tearing my knuckles punching trees and parking meters, drunk and enraged, and always with an audience.

"Stay clear of him. He's fucking crazy."

"No, no. He's a poet. He feels things deeply."

Those were the responses I counted on. The men and most of the women turned away. Almost always some young woman pitied me and took me to her bed.

What kind of father would I have been?

I went downstairs. It was quiet, the television off. My father was just taking off his glasses and putting aside my picture.

chapter seventeen

1990

ON THE DAY before Thanksgiving, Interstate 86 through Connecticut is jammed. Veronica, three years old, is crying in the back seat. "Daddy, I have to pee! I have to pee!"

Robert, seven, is whining. "When are we gonna be there?"

We've been on the road for nearly six hours and we're barely halfway there. There's no sense in turning back; the traffic's just as heavy in the other direction.

"Jeez! Why does Poppop have to live so far away?" asks Robert.

"I peed in my pants! I'm all wet! Daddy, I peed in my pants!"

AFTER THE TIME I'd spent with him in Allentown, I didn't hear from my father for six weeks. I thought the weekend had brought us closer together, but as his silence dragged on, I kept going over those three days. Just as he had taught me to review whole ball games for the missed bunt, the almost double play, or the poor judgment of an outfielder, which had determined the final score, I was looking for things that had gone wrong. The trouble was that I didn't know whether the game had been won or lost.

I had known my father as two irreconcilable men for so long that I returned to thinking of him that way. I told myself that I had spoken to one of my two fathers while the other wept. It was as if, cleft in his image, the ferocious son had held the cruel and sneering father to account while the gentle son looked on in pity for the kindly father who, in failing him, had also failed himself.

Mostly I filled the silence with shame. I was an overgrown adolescent whose rebellion had been avoided for as long as possible. I had been a coward, waiting for time to weaken him. I kept seeing my father's tear-streaked face and clenched teeth. I had turned the tables on him and grabbed him by the back of the neck and marched him back to a mess he needed to clean up. I had invaded his peace. I had taken out my fury at Tom on him because he was a safer and easier target. I had been unfair, and I had wronged him.

Then one night he called.

"Dick? Your dad."

"How are you?"

"Not bad. Not bad. How about you? How are the kids?"

"We're all okay." I felt the old impulse to comb my memory for some news about the kids, a comical incident, a milestone, a recent adventure, and I resisted.

Silence.

"Dad?"

"Yeah, yeah. I'm here."

"That was a hard time we had together back in June."

More silence, then a long, whistling sigh.

"Yes. It was. Are we all right now? The two of us. You and me."

"Yeah, I think so. I was worried when I didn't hear from you."

"Same here."

"I just don't want to be the one to call all the time. We get into this 'Sonny boy never calls home anymore stuff.' Let's just call each other when we want to talk, okay? You call me too."

"I did. But yeah, yeah. I know what you mean. I will. I'll call."

"Me too."

"Well, listen. I've been giving this a lot of thought. I want to give you something. And your brother Joe. You both get the same. I want to be fair. I've been putting away a little money from time to time so I'd have something to leave you when my time comes. But hell, I plan to be around a while and you're better off with it now while your kids are little. But you gotta realize that this is it. There's no other money. So when I'm gone I don't want you cursing the old bastard for not leaving you anything, 'cause I'm giving it to you now, okay?"

"You don't need to do that."

"How the hell do you know what I need to do?"

"I didn't mean it like that."

"Well just don't tell me what I need to do or don't need to do. You take care of those two kids. You worry about telling them what to do and what not to do, not me, okay?"

"Okay. I just don't want your money, that's all." I could see his face, his exasperation with me.

"Will you just let me do this, damn it! This is what I want to do. Christ, you'd think a father never helped his kids out before. Or are you too proud to let me have the satisfaction?"

"Whoa. Hold it. It's got nothing to do with that." I was lying, or at least not being entirely truthful, even with myself. Because I wasn't sure yet where we stood with each other, I wasn't sure what the money *meant*. To either of us.

"Well then?"

" 'Well then' what?"

"Well then what's your problem? You're gonna tell me you don't need the money? You got two kids. You're paying rent every month. Whatever comes in goes out. You don't own nothing. You live in somebody else's house. As far as I can tell, you don't have a pot to piss in. So what's your problem? Tell me. I thought you wanted us to be straight with each other."

"I am being straight with you. I just need to think. Since when are you so loaded?"

"Me? Hell. Since I retired I sit here on my ass and watch TV and every month the mailman brings me three more checks: my back pay, my pension, and my social security. And I put some money away, in the bank, not much, but it adds up. Listen. If I don't give it to you now and I run into problems later on, with my health or something, it'll all go down the toilet. They take your last red cent before the Medicaid or Medicare, or whatever the hell it is, kicks in. You read about it all the time. Poor people work their asses off a whole life long and then get sick and, boom, it's gone. They take your home and every last red cent you got. I want you and your brother to have whatever money there is, or else what did I bust my ass for all those years?"

"Dad?"

"What?"

"What if we talk about this at Thanksgiving? I was thinking maybe we'd come and see you."

"The four of you?"

"Yeah. Just let me check with Kathi. As far as I know we haven't made any plans."

"That would be great. Really. That would be great. I think that Kitty's having one of her shindigs again this year, with all the daughters and husbands and grandkids. And Uncle Eddie and Althea and your cousin Eddie will probably be there. Oh, hell, you got second cousins you never even met. That would be great. I don't think any of your cousins ever met your little girl. And Robert was too little to remember any of them, probably. That would be great. Really. You let me know so I can tell Kitty to expect you."

"I'll give you a call in a couple of days."

"All right. You let me know."

"Okay, I will. Take care."

"You too."

"Good bye."

"Okay. Good night."

As it turned out, Kathi decided not to come. She said she had too much work to do. "But if you absolutely need me to, I will," she added.

"No. Not if you don't want to."

"You go. Have a good time. Say hello for me."

WE CROSS THE Hudson River into New Jersey and onto the Garden State Parkway. At the rest area, there are lines for the bathrooms, lines for the telephones, lines for food. We need all three. Standing in the men's room line, I ask a custodian pushing a cart full of cleaning supplies if I can have one of his brown plastic bags to put Veronica's wet clothes in. He refuses me. Robert wants to play video games, and he sulks and pouts when I won't give him any quarters. Veronica is overwhelmed. She reaches up. "Daddy, carry me!" She's soaked in urine, and I don't want her against my coat.

"Just hold my hand."

But she shrieks and starts punching my leg. In a moment she'll be on the floor, out of control, and I won't be able to manage her at all. I scoop her up. I'm angry. Robert renews his petitioning. The line is hardly moving.

"But Dad, why not?" he whines.

"Because I said so, damn it!"

Heads turn. Eyes look down. I put my hand on Robert's shoulder and he slaps it away.

"Leave me alone, you . . . you red-faced anger-man!"

After a few minutes of calming myself, my jacket hopelessly damp and sour, when we've shuffled a little closer to the men's room, I apologize to Robert for losing my patience.

"It's okay, Dad," he says. Veronica is asleep on my shoulder.

"You're a good kid, Robert."

"So can I?"

"No, I said."

Soon all three of us are crowded into a toilet stall. I'm kneeling on the floor. Veronica is asleep on her feet and leaning against me while I peel off her wet clothes. I ask Robert to go and bring us some wet paper towels. I'm in his way and he can't get the door open, so he crawls underneath. In a few moments, when he crawls back under the door with the wet towels, I thank him matter-of-factly, and he shrugs, proud of himself.

Outside the men's room is a wall of telephones, and I'm reminded I want to call my father, who no doubt expected us by now. I'm feeling burdened and impatient. Veronica is asleep and heavy, and I'm holding her wet and sour-smelling clothes in my other hand. Robert is standing in front of a vending machine that sells combs, aspirin, and magnetic black and white scotch-terriers.

"Robert," I say, "come on. I just want to get rid of these smelly clothes. Then we'll come back here and call home."

"Okay," he says, catching up to me. "Can I talk to Mom?"

"Huh? No. I'm sorry. I meant call Poppop to tell him why we're so late."

He looks confused and disappointed.

"But we can call Mom too. That's a good idea."

"Can I dial the number?"

"Sure."

At the crowded souvenir shop, I hold the clothes high, pinching together the ends to make a dangling sack. "Do you think I could have a plastic bag for my daughter's clothes? She, uh, soiled them." From under the counter, with its gum and candy and key chains and coffee mugs, comes a plastic bag. "I LOVE NEW JERSEY," it proclaims, a red heart for the verb.

ON THE PHONE my father says he's disappointed Kathi isn't coming. Actually, I'd told him earlier that she didn't think she could come. "She's swamped with work," I had told him. "She's got a ton of papers to grade, and this is about her only chance to catch up."

"She knows the whole story, don't she?"

"What do you mean?"

"Kathi. She knows all about you."

"Yeah, sure. I guess. I don't know what you mean."

"And she stayed with you through all of it, the booze and everything."

"Yes."

"And she knows about Tom and everything."

"Yes."

"And about your dad."

"Dad, it's all right."

"Your Aunt Kitty will be disappointed. Well, drive safe. See you soon."

"Dad?"

"Come on! Come on! Get on the road. You'll never get here."

"HEY, DAD!" ROBERT says. "Let's play that I'm-Me-and-you're-You game." It was our nonsense game, a kind of "Who's on first?" dialogue we often played in the car. I turn my head to check on Veronica; she has fallen asleep again, and I'm worried that she won't sleep tonight.

"Okay. You start."

"Okay. I'm Me and you're You."

"No. I'm Me. And you're You," I answer, playing the patient sage, pointing to each of us in turn.

"No! I'm Me. You're You!"

"No! How can I be You? You're You."

"You are! You're You!"

"Now wait a minute. We can't both be You."

"No! I am Me, Dad, and you are You."

"Okay. Okay. Now let me get this straight. According to you, I'm You, and according to me, you're You. We can't both be You!"

"I know that! I'm not You. I'm Me!"

"Impossible! I'm Me. We can't both be Me either!"

"We're not! You're You."

"See? There you go again!"

And so on, both of us laughing and pretending exasperation with the other's make-believe stupidity.

WE ARRIVE WELL after dark. Robert reaches up and rings the doorbell. I'm carrying Veronica because she's afraid of strange dogs; besides, she's just now waking, rubbing her eyes. I hear the back door open and close, and I know that my father has put the dog out into the backyard.

After a few moments the door opens, and my brother Joe is there, laughing his great booming laugh. "Come in! Come in!"

I shake his hand.

"I was just about ready to give up on you and go to bed," my father says, approaching from the kitchen. He has lost weight, and I feel happy to see him looking so good. Soon we're scratchy cheek to cheek, Veronica between us, Robert hugging him around the waist. When my father bends so Robert can kiss his cheek, I notice that his hair, cut short, has turned whiter and silkier, and that he has a strawberry birthmark on the back of his head that I never noticed before.

chapter eighteen

1990

THE NEXT DAY, as we walk up the steps to the porch, we can hear that Aunt Kitty's house is full of people. On the door is a cardboard cutout of the Horn of Plenty. My father walks over to the picture window, raps on it, and waves to someone inside. The front door opens, and my twin cousins, Ann Marie and Mary Anne, come out shrieking "Dickie!" and hug me and kiss my cheeks. Veronica is holding onto my leg, and Robert is looking embarrassed. My brother Joe and my father collect their hugs.

"And you must be Veronica," says Ann Marie. She squats, and her knees crack. "Agh!" she says. "I'm getting old!"

"Hah! Like hell you are," says Mary Anne. Joe laughs.

"Now let me see. How old are you?" Ann Marie asks Veronica, who stiffens and hides her face behind my leg. "Oh. You don't *know* how old you are? So how about you? How old are you now, Robert?"

"Seven," he says, looking down. My father puts a hand on his shoulder.

"My lord, you got so big!" says Mary Anne. "I'll bet you're gonna be a football player, huh?"

"My dad won't let me."

"Oh, he won't, eh? Well, we'll just have to work on him a little, won't we?" She winks at him and twists a knuckle into my ribs.

"Agh! Give me a hand here," says Ann Marie. She grabs my arm to pull herself up.

"I'm three," says Veronica, but nobody else hears her, because my aunt is standing in the doorway now, and from behind us my brother shouts, "Uh-oh. Here she is, the Queen Bee!"

My father makes a big fuss looking in the window. "What the hell," he says. "Just put some turkey in a paper bag for me to take home."

"What?" Aunt Kitty asks.

"There ain't no place to sit in there. You couldn't get another person in there with a crowbar."

"Go on," she says, stepping aside and laughing, "You get your big fat fanny in there and quit your damn complaining."

Robert and Joe are both laughing. Veronica is peering around my leg now, curious. My cousins flank my father and nudge him toward the door. Aunt Kitty takes my face in both her hands and gives me a kiss beside the mouth. She reaches down and with her right arm encircles Robert and pulls him to her for a hug.

"I'm three," Veronica says.

"You are? Well you are really something, I tell you, really something." Suddenly she's looking around; she checks behind her and says, "Where's Kathi?"

Everyone stops. I assumed my father had told her Kathi wasn't coming. I try to catch his eye but he wants nothing to do with this. I repeat that she's gotten behind in her work and needs these few days to catch up.

"Is everything all right?" But before I can answer she decides that we can't talk in front of the children. "No, never mind," she says, her finger at her lips. "We'll talk about it later."

"We're fine. Really."

"Let's go! Let's go!" my brother booms, clapping his belly. "Are we gonna eat or what?"

I pick up Veronica, and she presses her face into my collarbone as we crowd through the doorway into the teeming house.

I UNDERSTOOD MY aunt's question, what she meant by "everything" and "all right," and my response meant, "Yes, we're still together, and we plan to stay together." If she had asked if we were happy, I would not have known how to answer. It was true that Kathi had work to do over the holiday. It was also true that she needed some time alone, some peace; mainly, I think, she needed a rest from me.

"And she stayed with you through all of it, the booze and everything?" my father had asked. What a colossal abridgement that word "everything" represents to me now. Maybe it would have been easier for us if I had simply disappeared for the worst couple of years; instead, I was all too present, not only an emotional invalid in need of patience and care, but an unstable, explosive, accusatory, "red-faced anger-man" who saw rejection in every refusal and betrayal in every misunderstanding. I almost drove her away. Now we were both healing, glad to have survived, but exhausted.

Kathi had a dream once that we were walking through a varied and idyllic landscape, arms around each other, looking for somewhere to make love, and each time we found a place and lay down, a foul and menacing goat was suddenly there. It would snort and grunt and charge us, and we would flee, holding onto each other fearfully, searching again for shelter.

THE LIVING ROOM is full of people and the din of many conversations. Even when it's empty, this house seems crowded: every available space contains a figurine, a knick-knack, a doll, a china bell, a colored-glass medicine bottle. Or a plant: geraniums, chrysanthemums, African violets, ivy, spider plants, and ferns. Aunt Kitty is wading into the crush of bodies, making room for us in her wake. "Come on, make way, you hooligans. You can't eat if the cook can't make it to the kitchen!"

"Mommom? Mommom?" She stops and bends at the waist to listen to a cousin's child. "Can I please have a piece of candy?"

"No, not now. You'll spoil your supper. Give me your hand. We'll find you something." She turns to me. "What about your kids? Are they hungry?" Veronica turns in my arms and reaches for her. Surprised and pleased, she takes her from me. "Oh, you want to come with old Mommom, do you? What about you there, Robert? Come on in the kitchen if you're hungry."

"Hey, Dick!"

I turn, but it's my father who's being addressed. I find

myself standing with my cousins' husbands, in a semicircle in front of the television. They're watching football games. Henry, my cousin Margaret's husband, has the remote control in his hand, and he's switching back and forth. Bobby, my cousin Mary Anne's husband, greets me with a pat on the shoulder. "You look like a guy who could use a beer or something!"

"Coke. But actually, I'm fine."

"So when did you get here?"

"Last night."

"Hmmmm. Lotta traffic?"

"Murder."

"Hmmmm. How long did it take you?"

"Let's see. Nine. A little over nine hours."

"Get out. Nine hours?"

"Yeah."

"Now wait. It couldn't take you that long. What time did you leave?"

"Excuse me. Coming through." I step back against one of the tables that have been set end to end the whole length of the room, and Francie walks between us.

"Dick, you know Francie, don't you?"

"Oh, my lord!" she says. "Just let me take these pies into the kitchen, and I'll be back."

I can see my brother Joe, who is somewhere across the room, reflected in a mirrored rack of blown-glass figurines.

"Hey, Henry! Dickie's trying to tell me it took him nine hours to get down here from Boston!"

Henry calls back, "Glad you made it!" There's a roar from the fans on the television.

The doorbell rings. More people are pressing into the room. I don't know them, but it turns out they are my cousin Elizabeth's grown sons and daughters and their girlfriends and boyfriends. Veronica is tugging at my pants, and I bend to her.

"I got an apple!" she says.

Soon we're seated on both sides of the long continuous table that extends from just inside the front door through the living room and well into the middle room. My father is seated at the head and my aunt's chair is at the foot, nearest the kitchen, where the children have their own table. One of the older girls has been persuaded to preside there.

It's quiet at the table. I figure someone is going to say grace. Aunt Kitty walks in from the kitchen.

"Well, what are you waiting for?"

"We're waiting for you!"

"No, no! Don't wait for me! I'm still fussing in the kitchen. Eat!"

Then everyone's talking again and dishes are moving from hand to hand, back and forth across the table, white meat, dark meat, squash, potatoes baked and mashed, cranberry sauce, white bread and wheat bread, carrots, candied yams, corn, stuffing, butter, gravy, green beans, lima beans, and ham for those who don't like turkey.

"A ham!" my father says. "Hey, Kitty, what the hell," he calls out to her. "You're getting your holidays all mixed up! What's for dessert, chocolate bunnies?"

"You should taste that, Uncle Richard," says my cousin Margaret. "That's Aunt Dolly's recipe."

"Well pass it down here then!"

"I tried to make that cake that everybody always liked so much, that chocolate cake of hers? But it never comes out right. I don't know. I watched her make it once when

I was still a girl. She always said I could have the recipe, but every time I reminded her—for years!—she'd say, 'Oh, yeah, I keep meaning to send you that,' or 'I keep meaning to give that to your mother for you,' but she never did."

"Well, I'll see if I can find it for you."

"And see if you can find the recipe for those baked beans of hers, for me," says Mary Anne.

"Those beans!" says Ann Marie. "Do you remember how Daddy loved Aunt Dolly's beans? Good lord!"

"Yeah, but you didn't want to be around a half-hour later. Whew!" said Margaret.

"I'll bet they're up there in heaven right now," says Henry, "Dolly and Forrest. She's cooking her baked beans, and he's got a plate of them, washing them down with a bottle of beer."

"No. I don't think they'd let Forrest eat none of them there beans in heaven, not if they know what's good for them," Aunt Kitty says. "A piece of Dolly's chocolate cake, maybe, but not no beans. They'd have everybody begging to go to the other place!"

We all laugh together, and when we stop, it's quiet. I can hear the children in the kitchen. We give each other puzzled looks. It's as if someone's kicked the plug from an outlet.

"What the Sam Hill?" says Aunt Kitty.

"Pass the stuffing down here."

"Who wants mashed potatoes?"

"Is there any dark meat left?"

"I'm going to the kitchen. Anybody want something?"

"No. You sit down. Let me."

One of the children comes into the room. "Mommom?" he says. "Is it time for candy?"

"Are all of you finished your supper?"

"I think so."

"Oh, you think so. Well, you go back and sit down now. Mommom will be right there."

He runs back into the kitchen, and there's some arguing at the children's table.

"You see?" my father says. "You thought I was kidding. She thinks it's Easter! She's gonna give them jelly beans and chocolate bunnies. I don't know, Kitty. I think you must be getting old. You got your holidays mixed up."

"Oh, shush up." She goes to him and slaps him playfully on the shoulder. Now everyone's looking at them. She pinches his cheek, and he blushes and smiles as she says, "My baby brother. Giving his big sister such a hard time!"

IN THAT INSTANT I knew that she was the one who had shamed him into taking down his wedding pictures and the pictures of my brothers; the one who had said, "It looks like a god-damned mortuary in here." I was reminded once again that for all her Hummels and porcelain kittens and tinkly china bells, she is anything but a sentimentalist. I remembered my uncle Forrest.

I was fourteen or fifteen when he died. My memories of him are earlier than that. I remember making ice cream in a wooden churn with a red handle that he allowed me to turn but that I couldn't, hard as I tried, without his hand on top of mine. I remember begging him to take me fishing, and gathering worms for him. I remember his housepainter's brown leather shoes with wedding cake rosettes of plaster and paint all over them. And Bob and I rolling around in the back of his truck on tarps that smelled of paint and linseed oil. And turning the pages of giant books, bigger than either of us, books too heavy to lift, filled with pictures of flowers and birds and colorful patterns that people could choose from to cover their walls.

I remember the bluefish in a row on newspaper in the yard, the overpowering smell of them. Aunt Kitty was angry at "them there damn smelly fish guts." Bob and I stood at a little distance as Uncle Forrest inserted the point of a bowie knife in each fish and slit it up the belly. Some of them spilled open, something yellow falling out. "Roe," said Uncle Forrest. "Some people even eat this shit."

"You watch your language around them there boys!"

When he died, I was given his gear, since none of his five daughters fished. There were lots of old English books on trout and salmon fishing, with black-and-white photographs of men in knickers and tweed caps with wicker creels, smoking pipes and fishing with impossibly long cane rods. The spellings were odd. Fish-hooks were called angles. It was quaint and inviting and useless. To my knowledge, Uncle Forrest had never traveled abroad. The books seemed to be a kind of *Wind in the Willows* for grown-ups.

"I remember when he went in the hospital for the operation," my father once told me. "Cancer of the stomach. The operation was at noon, and by twelve-thirty he was in the Recovery Room. I remember Kitty was happy as a little kid. She's jumping up and down, saying things like 'It must not have been so bad! They must have nipped it in the bud!' and, Jesus, I didn't want to bust her bubble, but it wasn't hard to figure out. They opened him up and saw there wasn't nothing they could do. So I went with her to the doctor's office. Soon as we go in, she throws herself on the poor guy. 'Thank you, doctor! Thank you!

Thank you!' I'll never forget the look he gave me, over her shoulder. 'Mrs. Christman, please sit down,' he says, and she still doesn't get it. She's sitting up straight on the edge of her chair. Like I said, she's acting like a little kid, all excited, like she's next in line to get picked for something. And when he tells her what's what, she just stiffens right up, her mouth shut tight and trembling, no more tears, and she won't even let me touch her. But there's this moaning coming from her, even with her mouth shut tight. It's coming right from her chest, the damndest thing, right from her heart, I guess.

"So she took him home and took care of him, with a house full of kids, and Forrest upstairs, screaming sometimes for hours, screaming and shitting blood and holy Jesus what a mess. And I never saw her feeling sorry for herself. Never.

"When he died, she went out and got a job, boom, just like that. And she brought up her girls. And she still don't have no rest in her ass. She's always got to be visiting this one and that, or she's at bingo, or baby-sitting for one of her daughters. The woman will live to be a hundred."

DESSERT IS PUMPKIN, squash, cherry, lemon meringue, or mincemeat pie, or ice cream, or the chocolate cake my cousin Margaret has made without my mother's recipe.

Robert comes in from the kitchen and stands next to me, leaning on my shoulder.

"So, Robert," says John, Ann Marie's husband, "I'll bet you're a football player."

"No. My dad's afraid I'll get hurt."

"Now you played football, didn't you?" John says to

me. "Did you play after high school? When you went away to college?"

"No. I guess I just got interested in other things."

"In other things!" Aunt Kitty says. "Get the hell out. You were interested in the same thing you always was—the girls. Don't let your daddy kid you, Robert; he was busy chasing the girls. Ain't that right, Dickie? Tell the truth now."

"If Robert stays as handsome as he is now, he won't have to worry," says Mary Anne. "The girls will all be chasing him."

Robert and I look at each other. Both of us are blushing. I give him a squeeze, and he shrugs and goes back to the kitchen.

"Willy never liked the mincemeat that you get around here," says Francie. "When it was time for me to bake, he'd get in the truck and drive all the way to Quakertown to get the kind he liked."

Poor Francie: nobody picks up her cue, so there's no commemoration, only Henry, leaning back in his chair, saying, "God, I couldn't eat another bite." The men are patting their stomachs. The women are starting to clear the table. And the door to wherever the dead are is shut.

chapter nineteen

1990

I COME DOWNSTAIRS in the morning and my father is at the kitchen table reading the newspaper. The coffee machine is gurgling on the counter.

"Couple of minutes we'll have a good cup of Joe," he says, looking at me over his glasses.

"Smells good." I'm anxious to talk with him. This is the first chance we've had to be alone, and I'm worried we won't get to talk before the kids wake up. I ask him if my brother is still asleep.

"No. He went off to a doctor's appointment. He had these kidney stones a few weeks ago. He didn't want me to say nothing to you. He's all right now. This morning's just a checkup. He was in a lot of pain there for a while, until he passed them. Little calcium deposits, I guess they are. The doctor told him it was from the limestone in the water around here. He'll be back in an hour or two. Sounds like the coffee's ready. What do you take in it? Milk?"

"No. Nothing," I say. "Just black." I've turned a section of the newspaper toward me, and it happens to be the obituaries. "How bad can the water be?" I ask. "These two women both lived into their nineties. I think you ought to bottle some of this water; you'd make a fortune. Look —here's another one: eighty-eight."

"That's great if you have your memories," he says, pouring the coffee. "It ain't worth shit if you don't have your memories."

"Are you all right?"

"What do you mean? My health? I'm good. I'm good."

"You lost some weight."

"Oh, hell, yeah! Forty-two pounds. I'm walking five miles a day, and I don't eat nothing after five o'clock. That's all. Everything else is the same."

"You look great."

"Oh, Kitty keeps me busy. I put some new storms up for her. And the dog is good for me. He likes to get out and run. You want some toast or something?"

"No."

"So. I found out about Tom. He's living up in Whitehall. North of here. He got arrested. They arrested him."

"When was this?"

"Way back in seventy. You were in college."

"The year Mike died."

"Yeah, I guess that's right. I thought I remembered something like that. After you were here last time. Thinking about it, I mean."

"You mean back then."

"Huh?"

"You heard about Tom getting arrested right after it happened. Back in 1970."

"Yeah. I don't think I paid much attention to it."

"That was a hard year."

"Yeah."

"Do you know what happened to him? Did he go to jail?"

"Like I say, I don't remember, but I hear they convicted him. They called it 'contributing to the delinquency of a minor.' He wasn't allowed to coach anymore, and he had to go see a counselor or something. Anyway, he moved out of town. I know guys who know where he is."

"Fuck him," I say. My father flinches. "Leave him alone. I'm done with it. Contributing to the delinquency of a minor? Counseling? Give me a break. Fuck him." I wave my hand in disgust. "What time does the supermarket open?"

"Why?"

"I just want to buy a few things."

"Why? What do you need? I went shopping. I got cereal and milk and eggs and lunch meat and bread."

"I thought I'd try to make that cake, the one that Margaret was talking about yesterday."

THE NIGHT BEFORE, I lay awake upstairs in what had once been my bed, listening to my father snore. Robert was downstairs on the sofa; Veronica was sleeping on a cot next to me. It took me a long time to quiet myself. Just as I was about to fall asleep, my mother was there with me.

I don't believe in visitations from the dead. I believe in memory, desire, and a deep-down hunger for symmetry. So it didn't surprise me that along with my sense of my mother's presence came the feeling that it wasn't me, but her granddaughter, who slept with one arm dangling, her face turned away from me, whom she'd come to visit.

Veronica's birth had been difficult. Kathi labored long and hard, and during the last hour or so of pushing, she had sat on my lap. I alternated rubbing her lower back, slick with sweat, and, between contractions, twining my arms around her from behind and humming to her what I hoped was reassurance. She was in ferocious pain. The smell of blood was in my nostrils. My legs were numb. The nurses' voices suddenly became more urgent. Then the midwife spoke. "Girl," she said.

Later, with Kathi and Veronica both asleep, I headed for the hospital snack bar for a cup of coffee. I was wearing a T-shirt the nurses had given me: GLAD TO BE A DAD, it said. Heading back upstairs, I stepped into the elevator and found myself in a group of men. As we rose, the tallest of them, in a chalk-stripe suit, extended his hand to me.

"Congratulations!" He pumped my hand and held on to it, his other hand grasping my forearm. He looked around at the other men, who smiled and nodded, content to have him speak for them.

"What did you have? A boy or a girl?"

"A little girl," I said.

"All right!" he said, giving my hand a squeeze. "Got any other kids?"

"A boy," I said. "He's four."

"All right!" he said again, looking around at the others, his left hand moving to my shoulder. "Got it right the *first* time!" The others laughed.

I pulled my hand from his. The elevator doors opened. "Fuck you," I said. He looked stunned. He turned to the others. They shrugged and rolled their eyes. I stepped from the car and the doors closed behind me.

MY FATHER GETS up from the table, walks over to the counter, and returns with a card file and the coffeepot.

MIDNIGHT CAKE

INGREDIENTS

¾ cup shortening	2¼ cups flour
scant 2 cups sugar	½ teaspoon salt
3 eggs	1½ teaspoons soda
1½ cups boiling water	1½ teaspoons baking powder
¾ cup cocoa	1½ teaspoons vanilla

BOWL 1:
Cream shortening, adding sugar gradually, till fluffy. Blend in well-beaten eggs.

BOWL 2:
Slowly add hot water to cocoa and mix until smooth. Add vanilla.

BOWL 3:
Sift flour, salt, soda, powder together. Add to cream mixture (Bowl 1). Add cocoa mix (Bowl 2).

Whip to batter. Bake 350 to 375 for 30–35 minutes. Test with fork.

"There was something else we were going to talk about," my father says. When I look up from the recipe, he holds his hand up like a cop stopping traffic. "Just let me say this now. You need a place of your own, you and Kathi. I just want you to think about it. You don't have to say nothing. I know it's expensive up there, but prices are coming back down. You look at your finances, and if you think you can swing the mortgage, I want to help you with the down payment. Will you think about it and talk to Kathi about it?"

"Okay."

"And just start looking around. See if there's anything you like."

"Dad." Again I get the traffic cop. I reach across the table and knit my fingers with his. "Thanks."

VERONICA IS STANDING on a chair and stirring the batter. She's beginning to be comfortable with the dog indoors, although she monitors its every movement. Robert is in the living room, on the sofa, watching cartoons with my brother Joe.

I put the cake layers in the oven and walk into the living room licking my fingers. "You better hurry if you want some batter," I say to Robert.

He bolts into the kitchen. "Hey! Save some for me!"

I ask my brother how he's doing, and he tells me about his job. As he talks, I wonder why we haven't become better friends. It's as if our connection is based on loyalty, on our shared status as survivors, as if every sentence we utter has, appended to it, ". . . after all, you're the only brother I've got left." As if, in a world of disappearing brothers, all we dare ask of each other is to stay put, to remain reliably alive, thank you very much.

On the television there's an old Disney cartoon in which Goofy is assaulted by a hideous clown from behind a mirror. The mirror is the kind that turns on a horizontal axis, and Goofy tries to escape the lurid jack-in-the-box who chases him round and round the whirling mirror, mounted on a dresser with drawers that open and shut disgorging clothes that appear to be fleeing, until we see an alarm clock, personified and animated, wake and stretch and yawn. As the clock rubs its eyes, it notices Goofy's dire predicament, and rings and rings until he wakes.

"Are you all right?" Joe asks me.

"Yeah. Sure. Why?"

"I asked you about your job. How's it going?"

"Sorry. I got distracted by the TV."

"Daddy! Veronica's not sharing!"

"Umph," my father says with his mouth full. We're sitting around the kitchen table. "This is the one. Mmmmm."

"Can I have some more milk, Dad?" Robert asks.

"Me too," says Veronica.

chapter twenty

1990

THE CHILDREN ARE buckled into their seats, their windows rolled down so they can wave good-bye. I shake my brother's hand and embrace my father.

"Come and see us," I tell him.

"In the spring, in the spring," he says. "I hate like hell to drive all the way up there in the winter."

"Why don't you fly in a airplane, Poppop?" Robert asks.

"Nah," my father says, shaking his head.

"This time nobody will make you jump," I say, laughing. He hesitates for a moment, then joins me.

"I never yet *landed* in one of the damn things," he says, grinning.

"Good-bye."

"Remember what I said. You look around and get back to me."

"Thanks, Dad."

IT IS A brilliant fall day, sunny and cold, the trees magnificent against a clear blue sky, and I turn onto Sixth Street and down the hill to Jordan Park.

"Where we going?" Robert asks.

"Is that a river?" asks Veronica.

The playground is next to the ball field. Veronica runs to the swings, yelling "Push me, Daddy!" Robert climbs the ladder to the slide. I have come here again compelled by a perceived imbalance that puzzles me even as I give myself to its urgings. I am pushing Veronica in the swing, hearing the rhythmic squeaking of metal, feeling vacant and suddenly very tired.

Where's Robert? He's not on the slide. He's not on the monkey bars. Where is he? "Robert?" I call, holding back panic. "Robert?" Louder. "ROBERT!"

"Here I am!"

He has played a trick on us, burying himself in a pile of leaves.

"Don't do that! Ever. Don't you *ever* do that. Do you hear me?"

"Okay, okay, Dad. Jeez, I was just having fun!" He starts to cry.

"You're right. Don't cry. I'm sorry. I got scared. I'm sorry. Really. Don't cry." I'm on my knees and hugging him.

"Bet you can't catch me!" I say, and run back to Veronica, trapped in the safety swing, who is crying out to join us. As I lift her out and put her down, Robert tags me, a little too hard, on the rear.

"You're it!"

He runs to the ball field, and we chase him around the base paths. I'm careful not to catch him. Veronica has found a mound of leaves behind first base and is jumping in it. And I am laughing. I sit right down on the ground, and

I can't stop laughing. Tears are streaming down my cold cheeks.

"Boy, Dad, you must have thought of something pretty funny!" Robert says. He looks at me, puzzled. I can't stop. If I could, if I could stop the laughter, I would tell him this is not hilarity, but joy. Veronica yells, "Watch me again!" as she throws herself in the pile of leaves, believing she has made me laugh so hard. I go on laughing, crying, until I am finished.

"Come on," I say, standing and wiping my eyes. "It's time to go home."

Afterword

1996

> *"Memory is not only a victory over time,
> it is also a triumph over injustice."*
> —ELI WIESEL

I CHOSE TO begin *Half the House* not with the usual disclaimer one finds in the front of novels, but with what might be called a reclaimer, since it is the purpose of the book to reclaim all manner of lost things. It spells out the kind of non-fiction it is and sets forth the rules I followed.

> This is not a work of fiction. It contains no composite characters, no invented scenes. I have, in most instances, altered the names of persons outside my family. In one instance, on principle, I have not.

In other words, I drew the people in the book as I remembered them. I conducted no interviews. I did no research. I was telling a story I knew by heart.

And yet I did not always know it well enough to tell it truly.

When I was a boy, there was a time from about July to the middle of September when the water in the Jordan Creek was so clear you could see down several feet to the bottom. Especially when the sun had sunk low behind the trees, and there was no glare, you could lean over the bridge and look down and watch the trout and suckers and carp and sunfish until it got dark. If you spit—och-tooey!—a sunny or sometimes even a trout would rise to the surface to investigate.

Half the House was written over many years during similar brief seasons of clarity. Other times memory seemed frozen and impenetrable. There were also periods of torrential grief, which roiled the waters and changed where everything belonged, followed a while later by new understandings.

Some of the events in the book were written about many years after they happened and years before they found their right place in the story. Other events were recounted only a year or two after they occurred.

And of course, during all this time, there was a life to be led. And dying I had to stop doing. There was a marriage trying to survive "the booze and everything." And after a time there were my children, who needed more than a ghost-boy for a father, a wanderer of graveyards and old ball fields, a solitary fisherman seeking peace and calm.

There are "no invented scenes" in *Half the House* because none were necessary. For surreality, for downright weirdness, fact wins, hands down, every time. For example, on the very spot where Feifel first put a hook in my ice-cream cone, so to speak, and pulled me "right up out of [my] life, boom, just like that," there is now a triple-X video parlor. When I saw it, the hair went up on the back of my neck. I discovered this while I was still writing the book, too, but it was so exactly right that it would have seemed like fiction, and bad fiction at that. I had been working long and hard to fashion the world of the past into a text that would not only reflect that world, but do so on art's terms, with meaning carried in its correspondences and juxtapositions, its connections, its rhymes. And here was the world itself doing exactly that, it seemed, with no help from me! It was like a darker version of one of those children's stories in which, waking from a dream and rubbing his eyes in disappointment that the soaring eagle was a phantasm, the child discovers a feather floating down, alighting on the bedclothes.

It is easy, in retrospect, to see this as an omen, or as a message from the world, saying something like what Faulkner said, "The past is not dead. The past isn't even past." At the time, however, I just scratched my tingling scalp and drove on.

Then, on November 5, 1995, my father telephoned.

"The son of a bitch is back," was all he said at first.

"What do you mean?"

"Feifel. The god-damned snake. He's back. Coaching."

"Where?"

"Right here in Allentown! It don't look like he ever really stopped. They're going to pick him up tomorrow. They've got new charges on him, new kids, ten, eleven years old. Some of the mothers got hold of your book. They're going to nail the son of a bitch this time."

"This is unbelievable."

"It's true. Talk to your brother Joe sometime. He was in a bookstore the other day and some woman come in and walked right up to the cashier, no browsing around or nothing, and asked the guy for your book. Joe says she was whispering and looking around to see if anyone was watching, and she stuck it in her purse like it was pornography or something and ran right out. When he told me, I says, 'I'll bet that was one of the mothers.' Anyway, I talked to a buddy of mine who says they got a warrant. They're going to slap the cuffs on him tomorrow or the next day."

What I didn't know yet, because he hadn't told me, was that my father was the one who had put the book in the hands of a friend of his who headed the youth organization where it turned out that Feifel was coaching. My father's friend had spoken to the mothers of several boys who were often seen with him. One of them, it was true, was the woman my brother saw in the bookstore. But it was, in fact, my father who had set events in motion.

When I learned this, a few days later, I thanked him.

"I couldn't help it," he said to me on the phone. "I thought about these kids here. And I thought . . . I thought, what if you hadn't moved away? If you'd stayed in Allentown, then maybe Robert would have been on that team, and I thought, hell, does this snake get a crack at the next generation too?"

I was crying by then, leaning on the counter in the kitchen of the house he'd helped me buy.

"Man, I feel great!" my father was saying. "I feel fifty years younger!"

IT WAS THE decision, on principle, not to change the name Tom Feifel that proved to be fateful. There was simply no reason to protect him. I did not foresee anything like what happened. I had no incendiary intentions. I pictured him, if indeed he was still alive, as old and pathetic, living alone, surrounded by stacks of porn magazines.

I thought, more often, of some of my old teammates, none of whom I'd seen in decades. If Feifel fit the statistical profile, he had had hundreds of victims, and in fact I believe I know, thinking back, who many of them were. There was, I feel certain, the boy I called Scooter in the book, but there were many, many others as well.

T H E   D A Y   A F T E R the arrest, my brother Joe faxed the news article about it to my office. Below the headline, Feifel's photograph is next to mine, our framed faces side by side. When I saw his face, after more than thirty-five years, I started shaking, overcome by a wave of anger and revulsion.

My photo is the one a friend took for the jacket of my book; Feifel's has lines behind his head that look as if he's standing before a venetian blind. Of course, I suddenly understood, this is his lineup photo! The symmetry of those two faces seemed, for the moment, nothing less than the restoration of moral order in the world, the pans of the scales of justice balanced at last.

But in the midst of this giddy sensation that some miraculous event had occurred, something else was emerging. A disturbing question. How could this man have ravaged the childhoods of so many, hundreds it seemed, over a period that now appeared to span more than forty years?

W H E N   T H E   S T O R Y went out on the Associated Press wire, the police began receiving calls, from all over the country, from men in their forties, thirties, twenties, and of course from the parents of young boys who had recently been violated by Feifel. The numbers climbed. "We're at the tip of the iceberg with this," said Gerry Procanyn, the detective who arrested Feifel. "Those who have seen articles or who have purchased the book are calling to let us know that this is not something that happened just six months ago, that they were victims years ago. We've had calls from as far away as Florida."

Procanyn had been involved with both of Feifel's previous arrests. The first took place in 1967, the year I graduated from high school. (In *Half the House*, I recount a conversation with my father in which he told me that Feifel was arrested in 1970.

That information is incorrect, but it is not the date that matters in any case.) The charge was sodomy. The mother of the boy Feifel raped, however, chose not to put her child through the further trauma of a trial. The charge was reduced to disorderly conduct.

In 1984, during my mother's final illness, Feifel went before a judge again, this time on charges of "involuntary deviate sexual intercourse and corruption of a minor." He pleaded guilty to the lesser charge in return for a sentence of eighteen months' probation. He also agreed to seek counseling for his "problem."

IT IS HARD to use the word *evil* these days without incurring suspicion. It is as if we cannot believe anything with our whole hearts, and we devise ever more sophisticated-sounding ways to refrain from certainty and the action it will require. At what point does a healthy skepticism become moral incapacity? At what point is our professed confusion really cowardice? To use the word *evil*, outside a philosophical or literary discussion of "the problem of evil," is to risk being called a religionist or a right-wing reactionary.

For those of us who are neither, the discomfort arises from the mistaken conclusion that since there is no longer a single religious meaning we hold in common, then there are also no reliable meanings to be read in our histories, whether as individuals or communities.

Words are how we "come to terms" with experience. If the terms we use do not reflect reality, but hide and distort it, then our discourse, the community's ongoing conversation about itself, will be corrupted.

Within a day or two of Feifel's arrest, his attorney described him to the press as "a sixty-eight-year-old man with diabetes and a heart condition. He's also got another medical condition, I guess, called pedophilia."

When I read that statement, I was relieved. His lawyer was not protesting Feifel's innocence. At the same time, with the enormity of Feifel's devastation becoming clearer daily, I was moved to suggest to my brother Joe that Jeffrey Dahmer must have had a "medical condition, I guess." It's called cannibalism.

The word *pedophile* comes from Greek and means, literally, "one who loves children." What an Orwellian inversion.

The rape of a child is an act of violence and an expression of contempt, not of sexuality or affection. The term *pedophile* is more than a misnomer, however; a clinical—that is, pseudomedical—term, it asks us to see such evil as arising from disease or illness, evil in its effect, perhaps, but no more intentional than, say, muscular dystrophy. This makes the violation of children a part of the natural order and the perpetrator one who cannot help himself. On one of the few occasions when he spoke to a reporter, Feifel said, "They tell me it can't be controlled."

It may be hard, in our historical moment, to distinguish between misfortune and evil. Perhaps our century's manmade horrors, including the fear of all life's annihilation in a blast detonated by a human hand, has made the point seem moot.

It is not. To view avoidable suffering, caused by monstrous selfishness and an utter absence of empathy, as mere misfortune or a "medical condition," is to blame the gods and kick the victims to the curb. It is a betrayal of the very idea of the human and the ultimate capitulation to fatalism and despair.

At the same time, implicit in the view that people are responsible for their actions is the idea, which I, for one, cannot live without, that transformation is possible, that people can change. We are none of us merely good or evil, but our deeds are.

In place of the term *pedophile*, then, let me offer an alternative: *pedoscele*, from the Latin *scelus*, meaning "evil deed." Try it. *Pedoscele*: One who does evil to children.

If this kind of criminal is a genetic anomaly, or psychologically malformed (when in doubt, blame his mother), then the community itself bears no responsibility either to examine the social, political, and cultural forces that continue to give rise to such evil or to mete out justice, since the evil is, after all, a "medical" problem.

But if we understand Feifel's "disease," for the moment, as the analogy that it is rather than as a literal truth, then its "cure" lies not in gene splicing, new drugs, or even new understandings of abnormal psychology, but in changing the way that the culture views children, especially the systems of cruelty designed to turn boys into gladiators with nothing but contempt for weakness, which is in turn absurdly and derisively identified with all things female. Because the curriculum of cruelty, with its emphasis on obedience to authority, alienation from emotion, desensitization to pain, destruction of empathy, and worship of victory still prevails in the raising of boys, there will be more victims and more pedosceles, more Feifels.

I believe that the silence that allowed Feifel to extinguish the joy of so many is not a static but a dynamic silence. It required participation. Many knew. Fear, shame, cowardice, ignorance—all these things played a part. Some thought it merely "naughty." I have heard the word *diddle* used to describe (and dismiss) the violation of children, as in "He likes to diddle little boys." It is a word that seems made to order, silly sounding, sniggering. Playing around, fooling around, fucking around—great foggy euphemisms into which real children vanish.

Feifel behaved as if there were no such thing as justice, and for nearly forty years the community gave him no reason to believe otherwise. The silence that allowed him to violate what now appears to have been hundreds of children must be examined. If we describe it accurately, its roles and processes, its parts and mechanisms, it can serve as a template for understanding how the same silence works in other communities. Then we can begin to dismantle the structure of shame, lies, and fear that renders us blind to the suffering of so many children.

Half the house will have to come down.

SOON MY PHONE was ringing daily with calls from men across the country who were looking for help coming to terms with their own histories. Typically such calls would begin, "Hello? I'm not sure I've got the right Richard Hoffman. Are you the guy who wrote a book called *Half the House*? I gotta talk to you, man. I've never been able to tell anybody this."

The stories I heard then, outpourings of grief and rage, were almost more than I could bear. They told of camp counselors, priests, teachers, scoutmasters, coaches, uncles, fathers. Men with authority and power over children. And with continuing power, in the form of a paralyzing silence, over these men who were calling me now, who were finding speech after years, often decades, of mute suffering.

I kept a list of numbers next to the phone. Hotlines. Support groups. National organizations. After explaining that I was neither a therapist nor a law enforcement officer (often my first chance to speak came five or even ten minutes into the call), I listened. It was hardly necessary to say anything at all.

When you begin to speak, you disturb an inviolate wholeness, and you say what you can above the roar of forgetfulness wearing you down with its insistence on the inconsequential nature of your memories, sweeping you down the long flume into exhaustion and defeat. I remember the first time I tried to tell someone.

He was a psychiatrist, the head of the mental health department of a large health maintenance organization. I had not been seeing him very long, maybe two or three weeks. I'd been referred to him to do "grief work" a few months after my mother died. "I think this is important," I said. He said nothing, but made a note on his legal pad. My throat closed, and not only could I not get out the words, I could barely breathe. "Back," I said. "When I was ten. There was this coach."

When I finished telling the story, he slapped the pad and pen down on his desk and sneered at me. "Listen here, tinkerbell," he said, "enough of this. Either you decide that there was a little ass-fucking and cock-sucking back then and no big deal, or you can blow your brains out over it. So what's it gonna be?"

What it was gonna be was four blocks to the nearest bar. I had already tried the first alternative, and it had carried me as far as it would. I had a child, a son named after my brother Bobby. Blow my brains out? Scotch. Double. No ice.

Sometimes it was obvious the caller had been drinking. Sometimes I suggested dealing with that first. I gave out numbers.

But I often wondered myself if they'd called the right Richard Hoffman. I had written *Half the House* as a literary work; as such, it arose from and embodied multiple intentions. I had intended to write about grief and family and history. I wrote about the time and place I was born into, the ongoing conversation of one American community and how a child tried to make sense of it. I wanted to subvert tired pieties, move readers to pity and outrage, remember and revivify the dead. Now newspaper headlines were calling it a "sex abuse memoir" and a "book about molestation."

It seems to me that any work of personal history, in our Freud-shadowed age, is seen as a search for psychological relief. Applied to a literary work, this view tends to crowd out all others and becomes dismissive of more meaning than it makes. I suspect this is its function.

Soon after *Half the House* was published, and well before the arrest of Feifel, I was in a radio studio, about to be interviewed. As we prepared to begin, the interviewer told me that my book "must have been cathartic" for me. When I suggested that the term *catharsis*, before it was commandeered by psychology, was a literary term and that it stood for what the Greek dramatist tried to effect in their audience, not in themselves, I was told that I was full of it.

"Nonsense, Why else would you write such a book?" the interviewer said.

Flustered, I said that I wrote it because I am a writer and I had to. "Oh, give me a break," she said. A technician adjusted my microphone, and while he fumbled with a length of cord, taping it to the table, I told her that Camus once said in a radio interview that we make art "to save from death a living image of our passions and our sufferings." She was looking through a glass window at a technician using his fingers to count down from ten.

"So you think it's art?"

"Yes. Or I would not have published it."

"Well, I look forward to reading it." We were on the air. "My guest is Richard Hoffman, who has just published a book about his life called *Half the House*. So, tell us, Richard Hoffman: what's so special about your life that we should care enough about it to want to buy your book?"

"My book is not about my life," I said. It was one of those rare moments when panic produces clarity. "My book is about our life."

There is a simplistic notion, born of daytime television and pop psychology, that one tells the truth in order to unburden oneself, as if telling the truth could serve no other function. Not only is this wrong but it perpetuates a cruel delusion, as if all one has to do is vomit up, undigested, the bilious and bitter truth, and, ah, that's better. As if understanding how the past has shaped the present is of no importance. When people place their hope in such a mechanical view of their own humanity, they become fools on the road to despair. Telling the truth is an arduous process through which we accomplish not merely relief, but justice. The resistance to amnesia is a political commitment as well as a personal, literary, and spiritual one.

But all this talk of intention aside for a moment, what I learned from the stammering brave men who phoned me was something about the power of books and the inescapably political nature of art. I learned that our creations become creatures, living beings with agency and influence, the same way we ourselves accomplish this: by being born into the fallen world of time, of history.

A book is like a clock—a grandfather clock, maybe, handcrafted of oak with inlaid cherry and ash, brass pinecones, ship's bells, maybe even a gilded cuckoo—that tells those who read it the time, and each who reads it knows what it is time, in his or her own day, to do.

No one, however, taught me more about the power of the written word than an eleven-year-old boy named Michael. He was one of four boys selected by the district attorney from among many more to testify against Feifel. Later on, at the pretrial hearing, they would tell of threats and pornography and all manner of violation, all of it sickeningly familiar to me. Michael had last been assaulted by Feifel less than a month before the arrest. His mother, the woman whom my brother Joe had noticed in the bookstore, phoned to ask if I would call her son some evening. "It would mean a lot to him," she said.

It took me a few days to call. What could I say to him, a boy my son's age, who might have been myself some thirty-five years earlier? What had I needed to hear? I felt I had nothing to give him. I called. His mother answered and went to get him.

"Hello?"

"Michael?"

"Yeah."

"Michael, this is Richard Hoffman. I wanted to call you and see how you're doing."

"Yeah."

"How are you?"

"Okay."

This was going nowhere. "How are you doing in school? Is it hard right now with all this going on?"

"Nah."

"Is it hard to concentrate on schoolwork?"

"Nah. I do good in school. I mean well."

What did I have to say to him? "You're a brave kid, Michael. Do you know that?"

"Yeah."

I smiled and relaxed. This was familiar. I was talking to an eleven-year-old who was being talked to, or at, by a grown-up.

"Well, that's all I wanted to tell you, that I think you're a brave kid."

"Yeah."

"So hang in there, okay? I'll give you a call again sometime, okay?"

"Yeah. Um. Thanks."

"Sure," I said. "No problem."

"No. I mean thanks for, you know, for writing that book. You made it stop."

It.

Postscript:
Pictures of Boyhood[1]
New Rivers Press Edition
2005

" *Virtue consisted in winning; it consisted in being bigger, stronger, handsomer, richer, more popular, more elegant, more unscrupulous than other people—in dominating them, bullying them, making them suffer pain, making them look foolish, getting the better of them in every way. Life was hierarchical and whatever happened was right. There were the strong, who deserved to win and always did win, and there were the weak who deserved to lose and always did lose, everlastingly.* "

—GEORGE ORWELL
Such, Such Were the Joys

I HAVE TRIED to be done with this.

I am one of five boys in the picture. There is a ballpoint arrow coming down from the sky from outside the frame of the photo, and it points to me. I don't remember the names of two of the other four boys. We're all in baseball uniforms. Although the photograph is black and white, I remember that our caps were black with orange letters—NE for North End—and that the trim on our uniforms was a thin black and orange brocade. I don't remember this particular

---

[1] This essay first appeared in *The Literary Review*, Vol 45, #4, Summer, 2002.

day, although I know the spot where the photo was taken, just behind the handball courts at Jordan Park in Allentown, Pennsylvania. It is 1960 or 1961. How the photo, which was taken by coach Feifel, came to be in my possession, is a story in itself.

On June 20, 1997, "Dateline NBC" aired an eighteen-minute segment on *Half the House* and its impact. The program, shaped by "Dateline" correspondent John Hockenberry, was several weeks in the making and included lengthy interviews with me, with my father, and with Michael, one of Feifel's last victims, then 12 years old. The segment was completed nearly a year before it finally aired, a year largely given over to the O. J. Simpson trial.

On the third day following the broadcast, I came home to a message from Detective Gerry Procanyn saying, simply, "I thought you should know that Mr. Feifel died yesterday morning after two days in the hospital." In other words, he had been admitted to the prison hospital the morning after the "Dateline" broadcast. He was soon transferred to the local hospital, where he died.

I was immediately suspicious. I have worked as a volunteer in prison substance-abuse and violence-prevention programs. There isn't much to do in most prisons: lift weights, watch tv, and brutalize child rapists known as "skinners," "short-eyes," and a number of other terms.

I traveled to Pennsylvania to talk with Detective Procanyn who suggested we get together for breakfast. I thought I remembered where the diner was where we agreed to meet, but I left extra time in case I got lost. After all, more than thirty years had passed since I lived in that town. I got there early, of course. I sat in a booth where I could see the parking lot.

Gerry Procanyn was as I remembered him, short and

stocky, sporting a trim VanDyke. He was wearing a suit and tie a little out of fashion and cowboy boots. As he approached the diner from his car, he ran a comb through his white hair and patted it on one side.

We ordered our breakfasts and Procanyn wanted to talk about "the tv show," what he thought was good about it and what he wished they hadn't left out. "I showed them all the evidence we had, all the stuff we collected from his house," he said. "I think there's a real story there. You heard anything else from those guys? Because when they were here a couple of them were talking about a movie. I think this would make a great movie. Nobody said nothing to you about that?"

I shook my head.

"You don't hear from them at all anymore?"

I shook my head again.

He talked about his passion for restoring antique cars. Our food arrived. He asked about my dad whom he'd met at Feifel's sentencing. He talked about his girlfriend, said he thought they might come to Boston one day and would it be okay to give me a call. Eventually I was able to ask him if he could find out how Feifel died.

"The death certificate from the Commonwealth of Pennsylvania says that the deceased Mr. Feifel suffered heart failure." He was cutting a piece of ham; as he leaned forward and brought the fork to his mouth, he looked up as if to see if I'd noticed his change of tone.

"You don't buy it," I said.

His mouth was full. He shrugged, made a face. "That's what it says."

I poked at my homefries. I imagined Feifel watching the broadcast and understanding, really understanding, the nature of his crimes against children. Viewing his entire monstrous career compressed and focused in an eighteen-minute account, I told myself, might have been too much for his heart, stripped of the denial that had allowed it to go on beating. I wanted his depravity and his death to be instructive. I wanted to conscript his disfigured spirit to squat eternally, a gothic grotesque shouldering one pillar of a better future. I wanted to believe in a justice not administered by men but by conscience itself. I wanted him dead from the force of unobstructed truth, not a victim of murder.

"Remember that Mr. Feifel has living relatives." Gerry was holding his tomato juice in front of him as if he was about to make a toast.

"What do you mean?" It took me another moment before I understood what he meant: there was no way the state was going to invite a lawsuit from Feifel's family.

He drank his juice. "Richard, my friend," he wiped his lips on a napkin and leaned forward, gripping the table, "one day every person in this diner—you, me, everybody—will die of heart failure. Come on, finish up." He raised his hand and looked for the waitress. "We'll go up the station. I want to show you something."

At the station I saw for the first time the evidence the police had assembled for Feifel's trial. In addition to the pornography you'd expect, and the sex toys, (including a long, clear plastic tube I first thought was a bong, but was really a "penis pump") there were the "adult" comic books I remembered: *Popeye and Olive Oyl*, *Dagwood and Blondie*, even *Mickey and Minnie Mouse*. There were pictures of women with animals, and women penetrated by guns. I was about to turn away, to tell Gerry I'd had enough. What was the point of this anyway? Then he directed my attention to a long narrow box. "Have a look in there," he said. "I'll bet you'll find that interesting."

The box was filled with index cards. Each card had a picture of a young boy on it (unless the photo had fallen off), name, address, parents' phone, height, weight, and on the back, a coded system of notations about what acts Feifel had committed on each boy—when, where—amounting to, I guess, a cardcatalog of masturbatory memories, or else a kind of trophy case. (Later, trying to tell my brother Joe about it, I said that maybe if Feifel could have had each of us stuffed and mounted, he would have. That was the feeling anyway.)

Thumbing through the cards, which were chronologically ordered, I started to recognize names. I was shaking by the time I came to my card. I wasn't halfway through the box, not even close.

"What do you think?" Procanyn asked me.

I couldn't speak. I squeezed his arm, turned, walked out, and drove back to my father's house. Think? I have been thinking about that box for nearly five years now. It is the truth about child sexual abuse. In the face of talk about "man-boy love," about "child-abuse hysteria," about "witch-hunts," about "false memories," it is the truth. Inside it, in the darkness, are hundreds of boyhoods; inside it, in the silence, are hundreds of stories.

That is also how I came to have this photograph, printed for me by the police department's photo lab. The copy has a greenish tint to it that I don't remember from the original and is much larger. I don't think I can say why I asked for a copy; that arrow started me to shaking when I first held the small snapshot in my hand. I knew I should have it; simple as that.

W<small>ANTING TO BE</small> done with this story is a kind of denial. To "move on" seems, at least to me, to suggest that an entire chain of events, having come to some resolution, has now be come inconsequential, as if the hard fruit of those branching consequences does not arrive over and over in its season. To hold that a return to silence now would not also have consequences is denial as well. In fact, I believe it would be a kind of suicide to so radically refuse the story of my life.

A journal entry from the month after publication of my memoir, well before Feifel's arrest:

> The danger for me, after Half the House, is to retreat in fear and stop remembering, to strike a pose toward the past that calcifies it, as if it has now been successfully packaged, boxed, wrapped, with no further pain nor wisdom for me. The danger is that I have sealed the well, or re-sealed it, put the lid back on it and walked away. It doesn't matter when you seal the well, or even if you have ever unsealed it; when the well is sealed, you either begin your version of dying—a jerky choreography of compulsions and rationalizations—or you go off looking for someone else's water to steal.

I have, in fact, moved on; what I have not done is try to move *back*, to a time before I understood the truth of my boyhood. Slowly and uncertainly, I am moving forward, trying to understand the ways in which my own boyhood is representative of many others', how it was shaped by ideas and institutions that continue to enforce men's estrangement first from one another, then from themselves, and finally from women and children. To the extent that "manhood" is a set of anxieties not congruent with the needs and concerns of women and children, to just such an extent is manhood dangerous, even death-dealing.

I learned this from the men in the prison where I ran a weekly substance-abuse group for two years. Working toward release to a half-way house, many of these men were at last ready to face their lives honestly. They had much at stake. Many of them had been violated as boys. They were at the time living in an environment in which the threat of sexual violence was very real. Yet, sitting around a table in a windowless, cinder-block room, they spoke of women in ways that objectified and demeaned them, turned them into prey. Unable to move beyond the wall of gender, unable to empathize, several said that to be sexually victimized would mean that the abuser had robbed them of their *manhood*; others nodded silently. The idea of "manhood" was so strong that they could not see that sexual violence is the most elemental violation of one's humanity, regardless of one's gender.

When I first agreed to lead this group, the program was designed as an eight-week course called "Tools of Recovery." About the sixth week, after a great deal of grief expressed as anger, as blaming, as fantasized violence, one man, thundering and rising from his chair, suddenly became silent, sat, and, head in his arms on the table, wept. As if it were a signal of some kind, a permission granted, a brave act that could only be honored by honesty, the men began to talk about boyhood.

With each new group of men, I lengthened the program, until the course ran for twelve weeks. I learned to wait. Usually the tears and the truth arrived together.

THE OTHER BOYS in the photo are my teammates but not my friends. Of the four of them, I remember the names of only the two taller boys. I'll change them here and call them Kenny and Phil. It would not be improbable for either or both of them to have turned, immediately after this picture was taken, and thrown me to the ground right there on the asphalt parking lot, one or the other crying out, "Cherry belly!" while they sat on me and pulled out my shirtfront and smacked my stomach while I kicked and yelled until it was a mass of red welt. One or the other might finish by spitting down on my face, even saying, "What are you going to do about it?"

I have talked to many men who remember both getting and giving these "cherry bellies" and who seem to have accepted them as a normal feature of boyhood. That these assaults, which happened to me frequently, were a kind of rape is borne out by an incident a couple of years after this photo was taken, in ninth grade, on the bus to an "away" baseball game.

I had been subjected to the usual bullying, I suppose, because I can recall very clearly that my right arm hurt that day, my "pitching arm" I would have called it, though I was by no means one of our main pitchers; in fact, Kenny and Phil were our starters. I can see each of them on the mound. Nobody ever threw more overhand than Phil. His was a bizarre windmill of a delivery, more like a pitching machine than a baseball player. Kenny was what we called a "sidewinder;" he had a wicked fastball that cut across your body from left to right if you were a right-handed batter.

I can recall that painful knot between elbow and shoulder from their once-again-refreshed mark on me, kept black-and-blue and sore by knuckle punches there at every opportunity. To soothe the bruise by touching or rubbing it was the signal that would invite a fresh punch there.

Some time into the ride I discovered my glove was missing. Kenny and Phil were sitting two seats behind me along the back bench of the bus.

"Hey, Hoffman. Where's your glove?" No way I was going to turn around. There was a lot of laughter. "Should we give him his glove back?"

Kenny's voice: "Can't you see I'm not finished with it yet?"

"Me next! Me next!" More laughter.

After a while my glove came flying at me, smacking the side of my face. Something wet, viscous on my cheek. At first I thought they had all spit in it.

Now I see that I was targeted in a different way. After Feifel's violation I seemed marked in some way that was visible to other boys. I'm reminded of that Far-Side cartoon of the two deer: one has a target of concentric circles on his chest and the other says, "Bummer of a birthmark, Hal." Boys do not walk up to other boys who are passive, cringing, and sad and ask what's the matter. Not the boys in this picture; not the boys, adjacent strangers, with whom I passed my boyhood. I had a target on me.

The boys in the back of the bus knew that the adults riding up in front—our freshman baseball coach and the assistant principal, a priest—would have to disapprove if their behavior came to light. They also knew that their aggression was congruent with a set of manly virtues, martial virtues, really, that they had learned, chief among them the ability to nullify empathy. "How would *you* like it?" the outraged question asked by a woman—in our case most often a nun—asking us to take some lesson from our transgression, would be missing from the response of the aging warrior who was our high command, sitting up next to the driver, talking to the priest, his boss, and studiously not turning round. In fact, his ignorance was dependable. From time to time, if things got too loud, he would bellow, "Don't make me have to come back there!" What would he have done had their cruelty and my ignominy been brought inescapably to his attention?

On the day this photo was taken, if Feifel had offered

me a ride, I would have hesitated before saying no. I would have had to find another way to avoid Kenny and Phil, some way either to placate or elude them. Maybe this was the day, the day of this picture, when I was dragged to the creek and thrown in so that on my way home I had to make up a story about going deep for a fly ball in right field, running it down so intent on robbing the opposing batter of a home run that I kept right on going right over the retaining wall into the creek just as the ball smacked into the pocket of my glove. It seems I already understood how stories push against others' expectations, desires, needs: what they want to hear, not to mention how they might be made to take the shape of what I want to be true.

I don't know, can't know, whether I am imagining or remembering the sting of my own sweat in the corners of my eyes, the invisible cloud of heat when the big round trunk of the car is opened and the musical clinking and clonking of hickory baseball bats as the canvas duffel is thrown in, the fine brown dust in my nostrils as the trunk is closed—*whump.*

The park where this picture was taken was the closest thing I ever experienced to paradise. These days I go there when I return to Pennsylvania to visit my father. We walk his dog there. I have written about this already, about the creek, about the white roaring rapids above the bridge at 7th Street, the trout fanning in pools and eddies. Have I mentioned the benches along the creek, and the weeping willows' long fronds trailing on the surface of the cloud-capturing water? The red and blue damselflies we called matchsticks? The cool darkness under the bridge, the lacework of trembling light on its walls? The way that the echo there taught me that silence is sound stretched thin by time?

But paradise is a myth made necessary by its loss.

Paradise was simply the world, the real one. By the time this photograph was taken, however, I could only enjoy it alone, and after a while I even started to believe that my love for these sensual things was unmanly, that I was wrong to find pleasure in them. Certainly in the shrunken world of boyhood's approved concerns there was no place for simple delight. Sneers were in ample supply.

All summer you could find Tom sitting in his car, a '51 Chevy, in the lot near the swimming pool, not far from where this picture was taken. The radio played—*Come on, let's twist again, like we did last summer*—while Tom sat, left arm out the window, aviator sunglasses on, watching. Watching. I think now that down below the angle of our vision he was stroking himself, recalling encounters with some of us, fantasizing—and planning—encounters with others.

The boy in this picture, the boy I was, hands covering his crotch, seems to be asking "Why me?" Psychologists who study the behavior of men like Feifel suggest that the world of such a person is both obsessive and opportunistic. Far from simply stumbling into temptation, those who assault children generally position themselves where they will have continual access to them, and their crimes are the result of a single-minded calculus.

Our uniforms, the finest of any team in town, came complete with those baseball undershirts, white with colored sleeves, and major league style baseball socks with the high thin stirrup of the big leaguers, not those two-tone, low-down Little League socks that the other teams wore and that looked like the kind of socks Ty Cobb or Roger Hornsby wore back in ancient times. Tom bought the uniforms, clothed us, with what he earned at his foreman's job at the nearby shirt mill. He bought our bats, balls, catcher's equipment. We were his team. We wore our hats with NE on them proudly, unaware that we had been bought, too. Every kid in town saw those uniforms and wanted to play for us. Parents, thankful that "somebody cares enough to do something for these kids," mistook Feifel's reticence, his lack of eye contact, for modesty, or as embarrassment at their expressions of gratitude, and this meant to them that "his heart's in the right place," that he wasn't trying to make a reputation for himself, wasn't asking for their votes, their business, their money. "He does it for the kids." In our black-and-gold, spiffy uniforms ("your baseball suit" my mother called it) we flacked for Feifel as surely as the other teams who had the names of banks and beer distributors and bowling alleys stitched across the back of their shirts. The man knew his business, even if nobody else did.

Anna Salter, in her landmark study, *Transforming Trauma*, quotes one predator as saying,

> " I guess it's hard to, it's really hard to say how you decide what child is appealing to you because, say, if you've got a group of 25 kids, you might find nine that are appealing, well, you're not going to get all nine of them, but just by looking you've decided just from the looks what nine you want. Then you start looking at the family backgrounds. You find out all you can about them, and then you find out which ones are the most accessible, and eventually you get it down to the one that you think is the easiest target, and that's who you do." [2]

There is no question about it. I am, in the photo, hardly

[2] Salter, *Transforming Trauma*, p. 63

there. My posture shrinks from the camera's attention. I had contracted; somehow I no longer came all the way to my skin. I saw the world as if from deep within a cave. I was like a gangster who will sit only facing the door with his back to the wall. I mean this as a metaphysical position I'd assumed: call it mistrust, call it fear, call it alienation. I am hardly there. I had been emptied, gutted like a fish. I had forgotten myself. I had begun to assemble myself, piecemeal, as I would be thereafter, trying on this man's scowl, that man's walk.

As a boy, I loved the story of the child martyr Tarsisius. A Roman boy, he had been entrusted by the persecuted early Christian community to carry the consecrated Eucharist to a catacomb where, among the hidden faithful, the word made flesh would be consumed. On the way there, he was accosted by thugs who demanded to see what he was carrying under his cloak. "Next to his heart," the nuns said. The bullies beat him savagely but he would not surrender the tiny incarnation of the divine that had been entrusted to him.

I was trying to be good. I was devout in my prayers, obsessive in my observance of the liturgy (gilded pages of exquisite thinness, purple grosgrain ribbon, every single day with its feasts and prayers and colors of the priest's vestments and place in the seasons of the liturgical year) trying to be the best altarboy at St. Francis of Assisi school. "What are ya, buckin' for—sainthood?" my father would say, a locution that makes me smile but also opens the doors of history to me— the world of my parents, the scarred consciousness of their generation with its critical mass of trauma survivors, raised in the Great Depression, sent off to the butchery of World War II, ready on their return to settle for any rung in the hierarchy except the bottom-most, any drug for the pain, any empty promise about the future.

I remember my ninth-grade music teacher, a former bandleader in the Marines. One day when I was especially pleased with having mastered *The Merry Widow Waltz* on my trombone, he leaned into my face with his teeth gritted and a sneer curling his lip. "You think you're some pretty bird. Oh you're so smart! Oh you can do it all! You preen all day because you can sing. Because you think you can fly. Well let me tell you. Your song's the same as any other: you sing for your supper. And you aren't flying anywhere. You're right here in the cage. With the rest of us. Get it?"

I learned nothing the year this photograph was taken, not even the things that mattered to me, like how to throw a curveball or how to pop a wheely on my bicycle or the *Confiteor* and *Suscipe* in Latin that would qualify me to serve at the altar even though I knew I was unworthy. Nothing would stay in my head. There was nothing wrong with my eyes, but the world was out of focus. I was the kid walking down the street staring into the middle distance, waking when a carhorn warned me to snap out of it. I'm lucky I didn't get killed.

Worse, I could no longer play baseball. Oh, I could field all right, and throw; but at the plate I "stepped in the bucket," down the third-base line instead of into the pitch. To some extent I think my debilitating fear was in response to a physical injury, although my constant state of distraction may have been the cause of it. I'd been beaned was the problem. I hadn't been wearing a helmet and the ball hit me on the left cheek and I went down and then, oh, man! it hurt. It hurt like hell even with an icepack on it. So after that, no matter how many fantasy homers I hit in my backyard, no matter how much excited commentary I supplied for my imaginary triumphs—*And the crowd is on its feet! It's going...going... gone!*—I kept "stepping in the bucket," down the third base line, afraid; "bailing out" we sometimes called it, and I struck out over and over again. I went from the starting lineup to the bench and stayed there. Finally, I quit and joined a rag-tag team without uniforms run by the Police Athletic League.

Marty Romig was a cop, although I didn't know anything about him in that respect. I seem to recall something about his having had a motorcycle accident on a slick road and that's why he was no longer in uniform. Instead he ran—he was—the Police Athletic League, or PAL.

He spent Saturday mornings gathering us together from all over town, collecting bundles of old newspapers and rags in the process. It was a big, dark blue delivery truck with the PAL insignia on the side, a police badge with PAL inside it, the same badge sewn on the peaks of our caps. This ongoing paper drive was how the program bought balls and bats and caps. I remember the stamped metal floor of the truck, and how we spent all morning wrestling one another on its waffled surface as the space shrank, filling with bundles of newspapers and magazines.

Marty was no baseball player. I remember him pitching batting practice with no form or grace to speak of, no *oomph* on the ball, and not much control either. Marty was a bowler. His right forearm looked like Popeye's. That whole right forearm and hand were so hypertrophied that his left looked withered by comparison.

This was around the time that some kids were starting to throw a roundhouse curve, and it was humiliating when I ducked or stepped away from a ball that curved down and across the plate for a strike. I had had enough jeers. I was primed for self-hatred, and now I turned it on myself. I was a disgrace. I was a coward. I was a phony.

One day Marty asked me to stick around after practice.

Just me. I remember I was bringing in second base. That was always the signal for the end of practice, when Marty would call out, "Okay, that's it; bring in the bags!"

He squeezed my shoulder. "Don't go anywhere. We're going to try something, just you and me."

I dropped the dusty base, picked it up, dropped my glove, bent to pick it up and tripped on the canvas strap hanging down from the base. My face was hot and dust was in my eyes.

"I can't, coach. I have to get home." My throat was tight as when I put my fingers down it to make myself throw up so my mother would let me skip school.

The next Saturday, he ended practice just as I was about to embarrass myself again at batting practice. "You stay," he said.

When the other boys had gone, he took me by the elbow, walked me to home plate. "Tell you what," he said. "Put the bat down a minute." Then he drew a line with the toe of his shoe. (He didn't wear baseball spikes, or even sneakers, just plain black oxfords and sagging trousers he stepped on at the heel.) "Now when I throw the ball, I want you to step down this line with your left foot. That's all. Just step. Ready?"

He backed up only about six or eight feet before he lobbed one past me. Underhand. Then another. And another. At first it was easy. I didn't look at the ball. I looked down at my foot. After a while I looked at the ball and still managed to step along the line, toward the pitcher, not the third-baseman. Marty backed up a little each time. Every 15 or 20 pitches I gathered up the balls and threw them back to him.

"Okay," he said. "Pick up your bat. Don't swing though. Not till I say. Just keep stepping along that line." The ball went by at nearly a normal speed. I stepped along the line. Again.

Again. I wanted to swing so badly I could have screamed. Finally, he gave his permission.

"Crack!" I had forgotten how good it felt to hit the ball. Again, "Crack!"

I might easily have been left, if it were not for Marty, believing that adults all wanted something from me, no matter how they presented themselves, and that whatever I wanted or needed I was going to have to get for myself, without help, and probably at someone else's expense. I don't know anything about how he helped other kids, though I believe he must have. What I know for sure was that he cared about a frightened, eleven-year-old boy enough to help him overcome one fear that he knew about, and at least one other that he didn't.

That fall I showed up for football, of course. It was one thing to quit Tom's baseball team, quite another to quit his Downtown Youth Center Bears, perennial champs of the 110-lb. league. To lack the "balls" to stick it out on Tom's football team was a disgrace impossible to live down.

There was a drill most of us were unwilling to admit we dreaded called "bull-in-the-ring." Twelve or fifteen players would form a tight circle and count off. Then Feifel would call out a number and that boy would jog into the center of the circle. Then he would bark out another number and that boy would charge and try to knock the boy in the center down. As soon as one charge was over, sometimes as the boy was still getting to his feet, Feifel would call out another number and let another "bull" into the ring. The boy in the center would have to whirl and be ready or he would get slammed, blindsided. You were there, in the ring, until Feifel decided you'd had enough. Often, after he'd administered the coup de grace by calling the number of a particularly ferocious favorite positioned directly behind the player struggling to his feet, he would step into the ring and help the boy up, taking off the kid's helmet, grabbing him behind the neck and pulling him forehead-to-forehead with him. "Damn good job. Damn good. Ya all right? Good. Get your helmet back on."

Disgrace loomed over us, always. One flinch or cringe and Feifel was likely to blow the whistle. "You're done. You don't wanna play. Turn in your uniform."

"No, coach, please. Please, coach. Give me another chance!"

"All right then. Show me what you're made of. Get back in there."

On only one occasion do I recall a boy who decided for himself that he'd had enough. He staggered away with Feifel yelling after him, "You come back here now or don't come back at all! You hear me?" The boy kept walking, weaving and wobbly, until he sat down under a tree near the parking lot, took off his helmet, and put his head in his hands, waiting there, an emblem of shame for the rest of us, for his father to come and pick him up. We never saw him again.

By the time I became a high school senior, I had remade myself, or at least constructed a new version of myself that hid the target. Looking back, the process seems no more complex than the ten or twelve panels that made up the cartoon ad for the Charles Atlas chest-expander on the back of nearly every comic book (on the inside back cover were mail order offers for telescopes, sea-monkeys, Chihuahuas, genuine rattlesnake rattles, jumping beans, and ant farms.) The skinny guy with the rounded shoulders and concave chest is on a towel at the beach with a dazzling young woman in a two-piece bathing suit. The bully comes along and kicks sand in his face and unlike most of the women I have had the luck to know, the object of this poor scarecrow's affections sneers at him and goes off on the arm of the grinning, armor-plated Neanderthal. Of course you know the story: our antihero buys the Charles Atlas chest-expander and transforms himself in the space of two panels into a radiant beachboy with an adoring young woman on each arm.

Before you decide that deconstructing an ad on the back of a comic book is a silly exercise, know this: I believed it. I believed it as surely as my mother believed a television and screen actor named Ronald Reagan who flacked for the Chesterfields that killed her at the age of 55. I believed it as surely as I believed that our spiritual father, Pius XII, whom we would later learn had betrayed the Jews of Rome to the Nazi ovens, was the benevolent presence of Christ-like gentleness whose countenance graced every classroom I'd ever sat in. I believed it as surely as I believed that I was responsible for every sin and shame, for keeping my own soul pure and innocent, from the age of seven, as I was instructed in accordance with the Baltimore Catechism, 3rd edition, memorized and delivered flawlessly upon examination under threat of being cracked across the knuckles with a wooden stick.

For two years, from 15 to 17, I daily disappeared into the basement where, in what had been the coal-bin, I weightlifted myself into an armored pose. My barbells were concrete poured into coffee cans, the bar between them a length of pipe. I constructed a system of pulleys to lift other cans of cement. I went at it with religious devotion. I gained forty pounds, all of it muscle.

In the final panels of the comic strip ad, the young man stands up to the cruel bully and regains his self-respect. Authenticated by a female caricature—"He's a REAL man!" she squeals—he beams with self-satisfaction. More often than not, however, the story unfolds differently.

Anybody who came out for the high school team for early practice in August and made it through the double workouts, the dozens of laps, the thousands of calisthenics, the blocking and tackling drills, the boot camp presided over by coaches riding the blocking sleds with whistles clenched between their teeth, growling at us that we were weaklings, queers, sissies, made the team. Anybody could wear the uniform of which we were so proud if he were simply tough enough to not quit.

I knew Teddy. He had once played, briefly, for Tom's football team, the Bears, but after having his lip cut open one day at practice, he quit. The word was that he'd needed stitches and wouldn't be back for a week or so, but that stretched out until it was clear he wasn't returning. Teddy was a chubby kid, knock-kneed, nervous; Feifel had always teased him mercilessly for having "titties."

"Sweat, you lard ass. You got titties like a sow. We're gonna buy you a brassiere for those titties."

I believe I was in college or had just graduated when my mother told me, on the telephone, that Teddy had taken his own life. "I don't know if you knew him. It said in the paper that he was on the football team the same year you were." I think I must have thought at the time that suicide was simply the final evidence of Teddy's cowardice or lack of character. I don't know, but I believe now that that is what I would have thought then. I don't remember having any feelings about it. Now I believe that he "came out" for football compromised by his having been a "quitter" and trying, as I was, to regain or recapture his self-respect and the respect of others. He was no good at football. He was not at all aggressive. He was soft and sweet. He simply refused, as a point of honor, to quit, no matter how many double-teamed tackles flattened him, no matter how many times he took a deliberate blow from someone's forearm to his Adam's apple that left him gasping and choking, no matter how disdained he was by the older members of the team. No doubt he consoled himself with the myth that he was simply being "hazed" by the upperclassmen on the team and that it was all a part of coming, eventually, to belong. But Teddy never belonged, and I believe now that the day when he found himself on the floor of the shower, pissed on by his teammates, the fuse of his ultimate despair was lit, a fuse that in his case was only a few short years long.

Too simplistic? Please, offer me another explanation. I pissed on that boy. I pissed on him to not be seen, to buy insurance, to not be him.

Could it be that every single one of us in the solitary storm of the shower felt the same need to not be the one victimized, each of us with a fear whose roar could drown out any scruples we might have had? Even Kenny, the cruelest among us? No. He was the instigator, but he was no more cruel than the rest of us. The evil, the ugliness, the cruelty arrived there that day carried by Kenny, our Lieutenant Calley, but we all took part.

Our collusion and our memories of the event, along with any questions about what it meant, or meant about us: about who we were, pretended to be, wanted to be, feared we were, coursed down the single drain in the center of our circular assault where now I remember Teddy sitting, face in his hands, sobbing as we left the showers, all of them, for him to turn off. "Last one out turns off the water!"

OUR MORAL EDUCATION requires that we feel shame about the things we have done to others, but a child who is made to feel shame *constantly* has no choice but to inhabit a defiance that refuses shame entirely. In this case the work of learning, of becoming a more sophisticated moral agent, is undermined and replaced with a slavish adherence to rules on the one hand, or a renegade sociopathy on the other, unless the child can find, and take, the difficult path of art with its balance of ritual and experiment, its satisfactions of symmetry (a kind of justice) and improvisation (a renewal of courage).

As a boy, I loved to paint and draw. My first paintings were the paint-by-number kind you could buy at the same hobby shop where I bought model planes, ships, cars to assemble with a tube of Testor's cement that you opened with a straight pin. All the scenes were exotic: a woman wearing a mantilla, a pagoda viewed through a foreground of cherry blossoms. It required an even more obsessive obedience than the schematic diagrams of the model aircraft carriers and submarines with their tiny people who had to be painted with a brush like a single eyelash under a magnifying glass held in a vise.

But I wanted to paint the things I had drawn, either from nature or memory, things that conveyed—if not accurately then at least satisfactorily—something I was either looking at or recalling. I might have continued in this vein—drawings and paintings of trout streams and weeping willows and the covered bridge that crossed the Little Lehigh, using the little plastic containers of paints from the paint-by-number kits and throwing away the numerical map, but one day my father brought home for me a bird's eye maple case of real oil paints. Weber colors they were called. They came in tubes, maybe fifteen of them, and you mixed them to make the color you were after, not a color that had a number and was on a sort of jigsaw-puzzle drawing by someone else. It was a miracle in my life. The smell of it, the smell of oil paint, of linseed oil, of turpentine, remains one of the sweetest scents in the world to me. I envy painters the scent of their studios and I don't understand why anyone would choose to paint in acrylics which only seem to me to be a kind of scentless, denatured oil paint.

Some of these paintings have survived and remain in the attic of my father's house. Among the landscapes and sports figures are religious paintings derived from the art instruction we received at St. Francis of Assisi School, especially a painting I did around the same time this photograph was taken. As an artifact of my childhood, it is as stunning to me, in its way, as this photograph. The painting is the precise expression of my deepest wish at the time. It is a panoramic landscape: three crosses on a hill, Jerusalem in the distance, soldiers and crowd tiny as the sailors on the model atomic submarine I'd painted the year before. The sky, swirls of gloomy gray, is full of angels—weeping and winged toddlers, really—and the father, the ancient-of-days, a white-bearded wizard, Rex Coelestis, is apoplectic with rage. Yellow bolts of lightning tear the clouds around him where he glares from on high at this atrocity:

How DARE you do this to my son!

I CAN RECALL hearing, when I was 12 or 13, that some coach or scout leader was arrested for "contributing to the delinquency and corruption of a minor." What this meant to me was that the world, if it ever discovered what Tom had done to me—and what he had convinced me we had done together—would see me now as a "juvenile delinquent." A "JD," as we called them, was someone who was headed for his just destiny—jail: first juvenile detention, then prison.

I was not about to admit I was such a character. In fact, I told everyone—my parents, my neighbors, the priest, the nuns—that I had a vocation and was going to be a priest. I had been "called." The nuns taught us that even among the many who wished to give themselves to God, "Many are called but few are chosen." A little bit, I have to say, like an arrow coming down from the sky and pointing at your head: *this one. There's something about this one.*

In any case, I hoped that this assertion on my part would cover the stench of my corruption. The charge suggested that an exploitative adult like Feifel only *contributed* to a minor's delinquency, meaning, I supposed, that there was something, some predisposition to delinquency that already existed in the child, something underway to which the adult was merely contributing, in relation to which the adult was merely an accomplice or accessory. In other words, the minor was responsible; the child was wrong; the adult had only abetted him—the crime was the child's and had less to do with any specific action than it did with a state of being: delinquency and corruption.

In a similar way, I set out to prove that I had not been changed by Feifel. The prevailing view, vile in its impact on innocent men, was that men who preyed upon young boys were attempting to "recruit" them to homosexuality. In fact, if you scratch the word corruption in this context, you will find this hateful misapprehension beneath it.

Feifel was booked on a charge of "sodomy and involuntary deviate sexual intercourse." The sodomy laws have since been struck down, at least in most states, because they are the chief instrument of persecution aimed at gay men. The charge of sodomy equates the rape of a child with gay sexuality, stirs biblical connotations, and cedes categorical ground to homophobes. To my horror, as Feifel was led away after his sentencing, the father of one of his young victims shook his fist and roared, "And we're going to get the rest of you faggots, too!" The consequences of such hatred include the continuing risk to all boys of sexual violence. Boys who are routinely using the term "faggot" as a slur by the time they are eight or nine years old cannot be expected to disclose that an adult male is exploiting them sexually, even if they do understand that something is wrong. Homophobia teaches them that the something that is wrong is them.

Those of us who are appalled at the criminalization of consensual adult sexual activity wince when anyone is charged with a crime of "deviance." So when the serial rape of children is seen as a kind of sexual deviance, a situation exists in which a person who has wielded immensely abusive power over one weaker than himself can somehow be viewed by those of liberal conscience as a kind of underdog persecuted by the state. Most people, fair-minded and tolerant, are paralyzed by this way of configuring the issue. Most people haven't thought very much about it at all, but when they do, when events demand that they do, they can't get very far, because these premises, the roots of the discussion, the way the issue is framed, the way the disk is formatted if you will, allows only the most circular "yes, but" thinking and the wringing of hands and helplessness we have seen time and again.

Daily now, the newspapers offer us demoralizing reports of children forced to bear on their bodies, and in their souls, a bitter knowledge that adults, with their state-of-the-art denial systems, refuse. The same papers are filled with pictures of men in dark suits with red ties planning conquest, men in religious vestments of this faith or that directing our attention to another world, and millionaire athletes arguing over money. To ask such men to turn their attention to the welfare of children feels like asking a tree to uproot itself, a stone to lift itself, a bomb to defuse itself. Still, there is no choice but to wait, though with much less confidence than I felt when counseling prisoners, for men to begin to tell the truth about boyhood.

Looking at this photograph, one might think that these boys in their baseball uniforms, in front of a handball court, with a Chevrolet behind them, are emblematic of that golden age of America, the years of prosperity after the Second World War. Their uniforms are spiffy. It's summer. Their coach is taking their picture.

They are studying how to choke off empathy. They are getting the hang of hatred. They are dividing the world into victors and victims. They are running a phallic gauntlet. They are dying inside, of fear.

They are learning the national pastime.

Photograph by: Thom Harrigan.

Richard Hoffman's prose and verse have appeared in numerous journals, including *Agni, Ascent, Harvard Review, Poetry,* and in anthologies. Among numerous awards, the most recent is *The Literary Review's* Charles Angoff Prize. He is Writer-in-Residence at Emerson College and teaches at the University of Southern Maine's Stonecoast MFA program.